Interpersonal Violence:
The Practice Series

Jon R. Conte, Series Editor

rpersonal Violence: The Practice Series is devoted to mental
th, social service, and allied professionals who confront daily
roblem of interpersonal violence. It is hoped that the knowl-
, professional experience, and high standards of practice of-
by the authors of these volumes may lead to the end of inter-
nal violence.

Legal
in Child
and

Legal Issues in Child Abuse and Neglect

John E. B. Myers

Interpersonal Violence:
The Practice Series

SAGE Publications
International Educational and Professional Publisher
Newbury Park   London   New Delhi

KF
9323
.M94
1992

For permission to reprint copyrighted material the author and publisher gratefully acknowledge the following:

Goodman, G. S., & Clarke-Stewart, A. (1991). Suggestibility in children's testimony: Implications for child sexual abuse investigations. In J. Doris (Ed.), *The suggestibility of children's recollections.* © 1991 by the American Psychological Association. Reprinted by permission

Spencer, J. R., & Flin, R. (1990). *The evidence of children: The law and the psychology.* © 1990 The Blackstone Press, London. Reprinted with permission.

For information address:

SAGE Publications, Inc.
2455 Teller Road
Newbury Park, California 91320

SAGE Publications Ltd.
6 Bonhill Street
London EC2A 4PU
United Kingdom

SAGE Publications India Pvt. Ltd.
M-32 Market
Greater Kailash I
New Delhi 110 048 India

Printed in the United States of America

Library of Congress Cataloging-in-Publication Data

Myers, John E. B.
    Legal issues in child abuse and neglect / John E. B. Myers.
        p. cm.   —(Interpersonal violence : The practice series)
    Includes bibliographical references and index.
    ISBN 0-8039-4231-1.   —ISBN 0-8039-4232-X (pbk.)
    1.   Child abuse—Law and legislation—United States—Tri al practice.   I. Title.   II. Series.
KF9323.M94   1992
344.73'03276—dc20
[347.3043276]   92-23604

92 93 94 95   10 9 8 7 6 5 4 3 2 1

Sage Production Editor: Judith L. Hunter

Contents

This book is dedicated to
the professionals on the front lines
of the child protection effort.

Acknowledgments

This book draws heavily on the experience, research, and writing of many people. I want to express particular appreciation to Mary Avery, Sandra Baker, Jan Bays, Judith Becker, Lucy Berliner, Linda Blick, Barbara Boat, Barbara Bonner, John Briere, Don Bross, Josephine Bulkley, David Chadwick, Jon Conte, David Corwin, Linda Damon, Debra Darro, Howard Davidson, Leonard Edwards, Harry Elias, Mark Everson, Kathleen Faller, Martin Finkel, David Finkelhor, Robyn Fivush, Rhona Flin, William Friedrich, Charles Gil, Eliana Gil, Gail Goodman, Beth Gould, Ann Haralambie, Stewart Hart, Robert Horowitz, Michael Jett, Susan Kelley, Jeff Kuhn, Kenneth Lanning, David Lloyd, Bob Masterson, Gary Melton, Nancy Perry, Theresa Reid, Michael Reinhart, Mimi Rose, Anna Salter, Karen Saywitz, Sandy Smith, Barbara Snow, Marge Steward, Nancy Stretch, Roland Summit, Patty Toth, Toby Tyler, Anne Graffam Walker, and Sue White.

Many thanks are due also to my research assistants, Cheri Simmons and Mark Tikosh, for hours of valuable work.

Finally, this book would not have been possible without the patience, love, and support of my wife, Laurie, and our sons, Eric and William.

Introduction

Professionals from social work, medicine, nursing, psychology, education, and related disciplines are aware of the increasing impact of law on their interaction with abused and neglected children. The purpose of this book is to familiarize professionals with the many legal implications of child abuse and neglect practice. It is not designed to provide legal advice; any reader in need of legal advice should consult an attorney.

It is my hope that this book will contribute in some small way to the continuing and vitally important efforts of professionals to protect abused and neglected children.

JOHN E. B. MYERS
Sacramento, California

1

Overview of the
American Legal System

Professionals from social work, psychology, medicine, nursing, education, and related disciplines carry the lion's share of responsibility for responding to the complex problem of child abuse and neglect. The law plays an important secondary role. The purposes of this chapter are to explore the workings of the legal system and to describe the myriad ways in which the law affects maltreated children, their families, and the professionals who interact with them. Increased understanding of the law can help professionals to interact more effectively with the legal system and can lower the communication barriers that so often separate judges, lawyers, and law enforcement officers from members of the helping professions. In light of the shared goals of all professionals working to protect children, increased communication is essential.

1

❑ The Adversary System of Justice

Disputes between individuals, and disputes between individuals and the government, are resolved in many ways. The vast majority of disagreements are disposed of informally through negotiation and compromise. Formal litigation in court "is society's last line of defense in the indispensable effort to secure the peaceful settlement of social conflicts" (Hart & McNaughton, 1958, p. 51). In the United States, litigation is based on the adversary system. This system is founded on the belief that the most effective way to arrive at just results in litigation is for each side of a controversy to present the evidence that is most favorable to its position, and to let a neutral judge or jury sift through the conflicting evidence and decide where the truth lies. In other words, the truth emerges from a clash of legal adversaries in the controlled environment of a courtroom.

Medical and mental health professionals often wonder at the adversary process, and find themselves saying, "These lawyers are certainly a strange lot. How can they expect to find the truth when they seem to spend half their time hiding it from each other and the other half obfuscating the facts with squabbles over inconsequential details?!" There is a kernel of truth in such criticism. Nevertheless, the adversary system—for all its shortcomings—has stood the test of time, and it leads to the truth in most cases.

A useful way to understand the gulf that sometimes separates attorneys from other professionals is to consider two hypothetical college graduates, Ms. Jones and Ms. Smith, both with the same major—psychology, for example—and similar interests, temperaments, and backgrounds. One goes to law school, and the other to graduate school in social work. From the first day of graduate school, the neophyte lawyer and social worker are embarked on *very* different journeys.

Ms. Smith's first social work class is "Introduction to Social Theory." The first 10 minutes are used for introductions, so students and teacher can get to know one another, and share a little of their backgrounds. The remainder of the hour is devoted to a lecture.

Across campus at the law school, the first class is "Contract Law," and the first words out of the professor's mouth are, "Ms. Jones, what are the facts in the case of *Hawkins v. McGee*?" (1929). For the next 50 minutes, the professor grills the terrified Ms. Jones with questions she cannot comprehend, and points out the flaws in each of her answers. When the professor finally asks the class, "Are there any questions?" no one has the temerity to speak. There is no lecture—just dialogue between the professor and Ms. Jones. After class, Ms. Jones is supported by new friends who say, "You did a wonderful job." To themselves, the friends thank heaven Ms. Jones was the target, and not them.

Ms. Smith's experience in the social work department was very different from Ms. Jones's in the law school. Ms. Jones and her colleagues got their first taste of the adversary system. They learned that their professor will force them to think critically under pressure, to analyze, question, argue, challenge, debate, and respond to criticism—in short, "to think like a lawyer." As a social worker, Ms. Smith has just as much need for critical thinking and rigorous analysis, but she learns these skills from a different perspective. The emphasis in the social work program is more on cooperation than on competition, on building bridges rather than on confrontation. From the first days of their professional lives, the social worker and the lawyer march to different drummers. Little wonder that at graduation, Ms. Smith, M.S.W., and Ms. Jones, J.D., seem to speak different languages.

Ms. Smith and Ms. Jones both love children, and decide to devote their careers to helping the victims of child abuse and neglect. Ms. Smith, the social worker, takes the plunge into child protective services, while Ms. Jones, the attorney, joins the child abuse unit of the district attorney's office. Not only must these young professionals struggle with the complexities of their new callings, they must learn to communicate with each other. Communication may be difficult, but communicate they must, because neither of them can achieve the goal of child protection without the cooperation and assistance of the other.

❑ The Judicial System

The work of American courts is divided between criminal and civil cases. Criminal litigation is instituted by federal and state prosecutors against individuals who are charged with violating criminal statutes. For example, every state has statutes making child abuse a crime.

A wide variety of legal proceedings fall under the category of civil litigation. Examples include divorce, child custody proceedings, personal injury litigation, and proceedings in juvenile court to protect abused and neglected children.

FEDERAL COURTS

In the United States there are two distinct, although sometimes overlapping, court systems: federal courts and state courts. The federal court system divides the United States into 13 judicial circuits. Circuits are subdivided into federal judicial districts. Every state has at least one federal judicial district, and more populous states have two or three. In the federal system, trial courts are called federal district courts, and trial judges are U.S. district court judges. District judges are assisted by U.S. magistrates. Magistrates exercise limited judicial authority under the supervision of district court judges (see Figure 1.1).

When the United States is a party to litigation, the government is represented by the U.S. attorney. There is one U.S. attorney for each federal judicial district, assisted by a staff of lawyers known as assistant U.S. attorneys. Although most criminal prosecution of child abuse occurs in state court, some prosecution occurs in federal court.

After a trial in federal district court, an appeal may be taken to the appropriate U.S. Circuit Court of Appeal. Judges of the circuit courts are called circuit court judges. The federal circuit courts of appeal have decided a number of very important child abuse cases (e.g., *Morgan v. Foretich*, 1988; *United States v. Iron Shell*, 1980).

At the pinnacle of the federal court system is the U.S. Supreme Court, which is the appellate court of last resort in the federal court system. The U.S. Supreme Court's appellate authority is not limited to the federal courts, however. The Supreme Court has the final word on the meaning of the U.S. Constitution, and to implement its authority as final arbiter of the U.S. Constitution, the Supreme Court has power to review state appellate court decisions interpreting the U.S. Constitution. When a state court misinterprets the U.S. Consti-

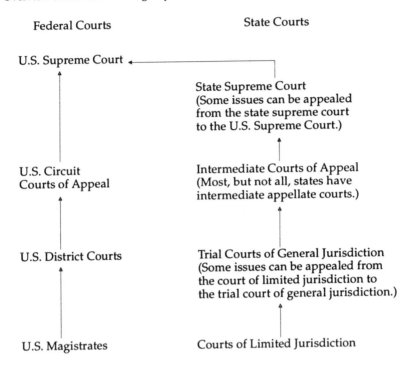

Figure 1.1. The American Judicial System

tution, the U.S. Supreme Court has the authority to correct the mistake.

The U.S. Supreme Court's authority to review state court decisions interpreting the U.S. Constitution explains why the U.S. Supreme Court, which is a federal court, sometimes renders the final decision in cases originating in state courts. The U.S. Supreme Court's decision in *Maryland v. Craig* (1990) is a good example. Ms. Craig was prosecuted and convicted in a Maryland state court of sexual abuse. At trial, several children testified via closed-circuit television. In her state court appeal, Ms. Craig's lawyer argued that permitting the children to testify outside Ms. Craig's physical presence violated the U.S. Constitution. Specifically, defense counsel argued that Ms. Craig's right to confront accusatory witnesses, guaranteed by the Sixth Amendment of the U.S. Constitution, was violated. The Maryland

Court of Appeals agreed, and reversed Ms. Craig's conviction. Because the state court had interpreted a provision of the U.S. Constitution, the U.S. Supreme Court had authority to review the case. The U.S. Supreme Court determined that the Maryland court misinterpreted the U.S. Constitution, and reversed the state court's decision. Thus a *federal* court reviewed and reversed a *state* court decision. (The decision in *Maryland v. Craig* is discussed in Chapter 6.)

STATE COURTS

Every state has a system of trial and appellate courts. Trial courts are the workhorses of the legal system, handling hundreds of thousands of cases every year. Every county or parish has a trial court of general jurisdiction that handles a wide variety of civil and criminal cases. Depending on the state, this court is called a superior court, district court, circuit court, county court, court of general sessions, or some other name. In rural areas, the court of general jurisdiction may have one judge, whereas a court located in a major city may have scores of judges.

> *Trial courts are the workhorses of the legal system, handling hundreds of thousands of cases every year.*

The trial court of general jurisdiction is complemented by a trial court of limited jurisdiction, which handles less serious criminal cases, such as misdemeanors, and civil cases involving relatively small amounts of money. The limited jurisdiction trial court may be called a city court, municipal court, or magistrate's court. In this book, the term *magistrate's court* is used to describe the court of limited jurisdiction. In addition to conducting trials of misdemeanor cases, the judges of the magistrate's court play an important role in felony cases. In many felony cases there is a preliminary hearing before a magistrate, who decides whether or not there is sufficient evidence to proceed to trial in the trial court of general jurisdiction.

Every state has some form of juvenile court. In some states—Hawaii and New York, for example—the court responsible for juvenile and other family law matters is called the family court. The juvenile court has authority over three categories of children: (a) delinquent youth (that is, minors who have violated criminal statutes), (b) status offenders (that is, children who have violated curfew ordinances, school attendance laws, statutes prohibiting underage drinking, and other laws governing conduct of minors), and (c) abused and neglected children.

States vary in the way they organize their juvenile courts. In most states the juvenile court is a component of the trial court of general jurisdiction. For example, in a rural county, the court of general jurisdiction may have one judge. The judge may set aside one morning a week for juvenile court matters. In a large metropolitan area of the same state there may be a separate building for the juvenile court, staffed by several full-time judges and support professionals.

Juvenile court proceedings to protect abused and neglected children are commenced when a document called a petition is filed with the juvenile court. The petition is usually drafted by an employee of a child protective services (CPS) agency, an intake worker of the juvenile court, or the district attorney or another government lawyer. The petition alleges that a child is abused or neglected and needs protection. It is delivered to the child's parents or other caretakers, and informs them that they must appear in juvenile court at a specified time to respond to the allegations of abuse or neglect.

To determine whether the allegations in the petition are true, an adjudicatory hearing is held in juvenile court. An adjudicatory hearing is a trial. Juvenile court adjudicatory hearings are usually less formal than trials in other courts; nevertheless, the proceedings are adversarial. The juvenile court judge presides, and the petitioning agency is represented by a government attorney. The parents often have their own attorney. In many cases, the child is represented by a guardian *ad litem*, who conducts an independent investigation of the case and makes a recommendation to the judge about the disposition that will be in the child's best interests (Duquette, 1990). As in other trials, witnesses, including experts, testify.

In most states there is no jury in juvenile court proceedings to protect children. After the judge considers all the evidence, he or she decides whether the child was abused or neglected. If the judge rules that abuse or neglect occurred, he or she enters a dispositional order determining, among other things, where the child will live and who will have legal custody of the child.

Another area of law that affects children is divorce and child custody. In most states, family law matters are the responsibility of the trial court of general jurisdiction. Allegations of child abuse or neglect sometimes arise in custody and visitation litigation, and such cases are resolved either in family law proceedings or in juvenile court (Edwards, 1987).

In most states, appeals from trial courts are taken to an intermediate appellate court. The final avenue of state appellate review is the state supreme court. In a number of sparsely populated states (e.g., Montana, North Dakota, Wyoming), there is no intermediate appellate court, and appeals go directly to the state supreme court.

❑ The Legal System in Operation

The legal system is immensely complex, with layer upon layer of statutes, regulations, procedures, and practices. The remainder of this chapter unravels this complexity by following the meanderings of a hypothetical incest case as it wends its way through the criminal justice system. Our hypothetical case involves 10-year-old Vickie Redding and her family. Vickie's father, Roger, is the alleged perpetrator. Vickie's mother is Beth. Vickie has a 16-year-old sister named Ruth. The Reddings live in a middle-class neighborhood. Both parents are professionals.

Not long ago, Vickie confided in her best friend that Vickie's father was molesting her. Although the friend was pledged to secrecy, she soon disclosed the secret to her own mother. In turn, the friend's mother telephoned Vickie's mother and repeated what she had learned. Shocked and confused, Beth scooped up Vickie and Ruth and headed for the pediatrician's office. The pediatrician examined Vickie and found medical evidence of sexual abuse. Once Vickie was assured that she could talk freely, she described a three-year history of molestation by her father, which began slowly and gradually progressed to intercourse. Vickie told the doctor that her father threatened her into silence by saying, "If you ever tell anyone, I'll go to jail, the family will break up, and you will be taken away from your mom and me forever." The physician informed Beth that she would have to file a report of suspected child abuse with CPS, and that Beth should plan on visits from CPS and the police. Beth gave her brother's address and phone number to the pediatrician, and told the doctor that the children would be taken to the brother's home until Beth could figure out what to do. At 4:00 p.m., the physician reported the abuse to CPS and provided the agency with the brother's address and phone number. That night, Roger returned from a business trip to find an empty house and no note.

At 6:30 that evening, a CPS emergency response worker interviewed Vickie, her mother, and Vickie's sister, Ruth. The interview took place at Beth's brother's home. The worker determined that Vickie probably had been molested by her father. Furthermore, Ruth disclosed that she too had been molested by Roger. Beth assured the worker that the children would be kept away from Roger. The worker determined that no CPS involvement was needed at that time. The worker informed Beth that a report would be filed with the police, and provided Beth a list of agencies that could provide information and counseling.

The Response of
the Criminal Justice System

The criminal justice system is not monolithic across the United States. Laws vary in detail from state to state, and day-to-day practices differ from one law enforcement agency to another. Exaggerating somewhat the differences among jurisdictions, a presidential commission remarked that "every village, town, county, city, and State has its own criminal justice system, and there is a Federal one as well. All of them operate somewhat alike. No two of them operate precisely alike" (President's Commission on Law Enforcement and Administration of Justice, 1968, p. 7). Although some of the actors, practices, and procedures vary from one jurisdiction to another, in most respects the criminal justice system follows a similar course from initial police involvement through ultimate resolution in the courts.

INITIAL POLICE INVESTIGATION

The Reddings' first encounter with the criminal justice system came with a knock at the door of the brother's home on the morning following Vickie's visit to the pediatrician. A uniformed police officer asked to speak to Vickie's mother. The officer informed Beth that CPS had notified the police of the possible molestation of Vickie and Ruth, and that the officer was assigned to investigate. The officer interviewed Beth, Vickie, and Ruth. Vickie and Ruth repeated their allegations of sexual abuse, and Beth said, "I can't understand how my husband could do such a thing, but I believe my daughters." The officer obtained Beth's permission to talk to the pediatrician. The officer discussed the case with the doctor over the phone, and the physician conveyed her impression that Vickie has been sexually abused. Finally, the officer checked Roger's name in the police department's computer, but found nothing.

ARREST AND BOOKING

The investigating officer returned to the police station and discussed the case with a detective from the sex crimes unit. The officers decided they had probable cause to arrest Roger for felony child abuse. A police officer must have probable cause to make an arrest. Probable cause is an important but vague legal concept. Basically, an officer has probable cause to arrest when he or she possesses enough trustworthy information to lead a reasonable person to believe a crime has been committed by a particular person.

The next step was to obtain a warrant for Roger's arrest. Law enforcement officers are not always required to obtain arrest warrants. In fact, most arrests are made without warrants. Generally speaking, a law enforcement officer may arrest without a warrant under two circumstances. First, an officer may arrest a person whom the officer observes committing a misdemeanor or a felony. Second, when an officer does not observe a crime in progress, the officer may arrest if he or she has probable cause to believe the suspect committed a felony. If the unobserved crime is a misdemeanor, a warrant must be obtained.

The detective filled out several forms, including a sworn affidavit, requesting a magistrate to issue an arrest warrant. The detective presented the forms to a magistrate, who reviewed them and decided there was probable cause to arrest Roger for child sexual abuse. The magistrate signed an arrest warrant and handed it to the detective.

Armed with the arrest warrant, the detective and the investigating officer arrived at Roger's home, where Roger was frantically trying to locate his family. The detective said, "Are you Roger Redding?" Roger replied, "Yes. What do you know?" The detective handed Roger a copy of the warrant and said, "Mr. Redding, you are under arrest for sexual abuse committed against your daughters. You will need to come with us to the police station." Roger slumped into a chair, dropped his head into his hands, and said, "Oh no. How did you find out?" The detective replied, "Find out what, Mr. Redding?" Roger said, "You know, about my daughters? I feel just sick about this."

Following Roger's initial statement to the police, which was carefully documented for use as evidence against him, the detective gave Roger the warnings required by the U.S. Supreme Court's decision in *Miranda v. Arizona* (1966), commonly known as the *Miranda* warnings. Roger was informed that he had a right to remain silent, and that anything he said could be used against him. He was told that he had a right to an attorney, and that if he could not afford an attorney, one would be appointed for him. After these warnings, Roger asked if he could call his lawyer. The detective said yes, and Roger's lawyer advised him to say nothing to the police. Roger informed the officers he would take his lawyer's advice and remain silent. Roger was handcuffed, searched, and taken to the police station. Once at the station, Roger went through booking procedures. His fingerprints and photograph were taken, he was searched more thoroughly, and he was placed in a holding cell.

THE DECISION TO FILE CHARGES

Following Roger's arrest and booking, the case was reviewed to determine whether to file formal charges. In some localities, prosecutors play a large role in deciding whether to file charges. In other locations, police and sheriff's officers make most initial charging decisions. In Roger's city, the district attorney's office makes filing decisions, and several hours after Roger's arrest, the detective presented the case to the deputy district attorney responsible for charging decisions in child abuse cases. The prosecutor reviewed the file and discussed the case with the detective.

Prosecutors consider many factors when deciding whether to file criminal charges. Of great importance is the strength of the evidence and the likelihood of successful prosecution. Also important are the nature of the crime and the harm inflicted on the victim. Based on available evidence and the seriousness of the charges against Roger, the prosecutor decided to file criminal charges. The prosecutor prepared a complaint describing the charges, and the detective signed the complaint and filed it with the magistrate's court.

THE INITIAL APPEARANCE IN COURT

A person who is arrested and charged with a crime must be taken before an impartial magistrate without unnecessary delay. Roger's initial appearance in court occurred the morning following his arrest. Roger's lawyer was in the courtroom when Roger was led in by a bailiff. As is usually the case, Roger's initial appearance was brief. The magistrate informed Roger of the charges against him and of his legal rights. The magistrate then advised Roger that the next step was a preliminary hearing, which was scheduled to be held two weeks later. After some discussion among the judge, Roger's attorney, and the prosecuting attorney, the judge set bail and ordered Roger not to live at home or to contact his children until further investigation revealed whether the children were at risk. In less than 15 minutes the hearing was over and Roger was escorted back to jail. Later that day, Roger's attorney arranged bail, and Roger was released from jail.

PRELIMINARY HEARING

In many states, a person accused of crime has a right to a preliminary hearing before a magistrate. The function of the preliminary hearing is to screen out cases where the evidence is so weak that the case should be dismissed without a trial. Although less formal than a trial, a preliminary hearing is an adversarial proceeding. The accused individual is present and represented by an attorney. The prosecutor must introduce enough evidence to convince the magistrate that there is probable cause to believe the accused person committed the crime. If the magistrate determines that the prosecutor's evidence establishes probable cause, the magistrate binds the case over for the next step in the process. In a small percentage of cases, the magistrate rules that the prosecutor's evidence does not establish probable cause, and the charges are dismissed. There is no jury at the preliminary hearing.

At the preliminary hearing, the prosecutor may call the child as a witness. Thus the preliminary hearing may be the child's first experience in testifying. If the magistrate binds the case over for trial, the child will probably have to testify again if a trial is held. When feasible, the prosecutor spares the child the trauma of testifying twice by using other witnesses to establish probable cause at the preliminary hearing.

In addition to the child, the prosecutor may ask professionals to testify at the preliminary hearing. As in testimony during a trial, the professional begins by answering the prosecutor's questions, and then, when the prosecutor is finished, the accused person's attorney has the right to cross-examine. (See Chapter 6 for discussion of cross-examination.)

Roger Redding's preliminary hearing occurred two weeks following his initial appearance before a magistrate. Vickie did not testify. The prosecutor presented the testimony of the pediatrician who examined Vickie and the police officer who conducted the initial investigation. Roger's attorney cross-examined both witnesses. The magistrate ruled that the testimony of the doctor and the officer established probable cause to believe Roger molested Vickie. The magistrate bound the case over for trial in the trial court of general jurisdiction.

THE INFORMATION

Following the preliminary hearing, the prosecutor drafted a document called an information, and filed it with the trial court of general jurisdiction where Roger's trial would take place. The information contained the charges against Roger and replaced the complaint that was issued prior to Roger's initial appearance in court.

GRAND JURY REVIEW AND INDICTMENT

In some states, felony prosecutions are screened by a grand jury. A grand jury consists of private citizens who are selected to review cases and decide whether charges should be filed. It is important to distinguish a grand jury from a petit jury. A petit jury is a group of citizens serving as jurors on a particular case. By contrast, members of the grand jury do not act as jurors on particular cases. Rather, the grand jury performs a function similar to that of a magistrate at a preliminary hearing. Like the magistrate, the grand jury screens cases in and out of the criminal justice system by deciding whether there is sufficient evidence to justify a trial. Unlike a preliminary hearing, however, which is an adversarial proceeding, with the accused individual and defense counsel present, the grand jury meets behind closed doors. Only the prosecutor presents evidence to the grand jury. The defendant has no right to appear before the grand jury in person or through counsel, and the defendant cannot present evidence to the grand jury.

If a majority of the grand jury members are satisfied that the prosecutor's evidence is sufficient to warrant a trial, the grand jury issues an indictment. The indictment, commonly called a *true bill*, contains a description of the charges against the indicted individual. The indictment is filed with the court where the trial will be held and takes the place of the original complaint. If a majority of the grand jury refuses to indict, the charges are dismissed. Some states use both the grand jury and the preliminary hearing.

In the state where Roger Redding was charged with child sexual abuse, the grand jury system is not in use. Thus Roger's case was not reviewed by a grand jury, and the charges against Roger were contained in the prosecutor's information.

ARRAIGNMENT

The next step in the criminal justice process is the arraignment. The accused individual, who is called the defendant, appears in court, and the judge informs the defendant of the charges contained in the information or indictment. The defendant then enters a plea of guilty or not guilty. In some circumstances, the judge permits the defendant to enter a plea of *nolo contendere*. This Latin phrase means "I will not contest it." In most respects, a *nolo contendere* plea has the same effect as a guilty plea. For example, the punishment following a *nolo* plea is usually the same as that following a guilty plea. The advantage to the defendant of a *nolo* plea is that the defendant does not formally admit guilt, and the *nolo* plea cannot be used as an admission of guilt in any subsequent civil litigation against the defendant. At Roger Redding's arraignment, he entered a plea of not guilty, and the judge set the matter for trial.

PLEA BARGAINING

The great majority of prosecutors engage in plea negotiation (plea bargaining) with defense attorneys representing accused individuals. In many cases, the result of plea bargaining is that the defendant pleads guilty to a less serious offense than was originally charged. For example, a person charged with a felony might plead guilty to a misdemeanor.

> *Due in large part to plea bargaining, some 70-90% of felony cases end in a guilty plea.*

In other cases, the defendant agrees to plead guilty to the original charge in exchange for the prosecutor's commitment to recommend leniency when the judge pronounces sentence. Due in large part to plea bargaining, some 70-90% of felony cases end in a guilty plea prior to trial (LaFave & Israel, 1991, p. 26).

In the Redding case, Roger's attorney and the prosecutor discussed the possibility of Roger pleading guilty to a less serious crime, but the prosecutor was unwilling to strike a deal that was acceptable to Roger, and plea bargaining broke down.

PRETRIAL DIVERSION

In many communities, individuals charged with certain crimes may be eligible for a program that diverts their cases away from prosecution and into some form of rehabilitation or treatment (LaFave

& Israel, 1991, p. 645). Participation in pretrial diversion depends on factors such as the nature and seriousness of the crime, whether the individual is a first-time offender, and the likelihood the individual will participate in and benefit from treatment. If the individual successfully completes treatment, the criminal charges may be dropped. Failure to complete treatment allows the prosecutor to proceed with prosecution on the original charges.

Roger Redding's attorney attempted to persuade the prosecutor to allow Roger to participate in the pretrial diversion program operating in Roger's community. Because of the seriousness of the charges, however, the prosecutor refused to authorize diversion for Roger. As is usually the case with diversion programs, the prosecutor has considerable discretion on whether to divert or prosecute.

PRETRIAL MOTIONS

When a case looks as though it will proceed to trial, the opposing attorneys often file pretrial motions requesting the judge to resolve selected legal issues prior to trial. Pretrial motions are often called motions *in limine*. For example, the prosecutor may file a pretrial motion requesting the judge to permit a child to testify via closed-circuit television so the child does not have to face the alleged perpetrator. Defense counsel might ask the judge to order a psychiatric evaluation of the child.

PREPARATION FOR TRIAL: DISCOVERY

During the weeks prior to trial, the attorneys prepare. The defendant's attorney interviews witnesses, talks to potential expert witnesses, and plans trial strategy. Defense counsel also engages in pretrial discovery. Discovery is a process that permits each party to litigation to learn about evidence possessed by the other party. The parameters of pretrial discovery vary from state to state. In general, the defense is allowed fairly broad discovery of documents and evidence under the control of the prosecutor. Under the U.S. Constitution, the prosecutor is obliged to disclose evidence that could exculpate the defendant. In some states, the defendant's attorney sends the prosecutor a document called a bill of particulars, which requests the prosecutor to provide details about charges against the defendant.

In addition to gaining access to records under the control of the prosecutor, the person accused of abuse may have a right to inspect records of professionals in private practice. The need of the defense lawyer to inspect records created by professionals in private practice is particularly great when the professional will testify at trial as a witness for the prosecution.

The prosecutor's right to pretrial discovery from the defense is generally narrower than the defendant's right to discovery from the prosecution. Limitations on discovery by the prosecutor arise primarily from the defendant's constitutional right against self-incrimination (LaFave & Israel, 1991, p. 860). Despite constitutional limitations on prosecution discovery, legislatures are expanding discovery by the prosecutor.

Professionals who interviewed or treated the child may be contacted by defense counsel or by investigators working for the defense. Before discussing a case with *anyone*, professionals should be clear about the affiliation of the individual seeking information. If the individual is a representative of the defense, the professional should consider several factors before discussing a case. Generally, professionals are under no legal obligation to communicate with the defense over the telephone, in person, or by letter. The defense attorney can obtain a subpoena that compels the professional to testify at a formal deposition or a trial, but absent a subpoena, the professional has the right to decide whether to communicate with defense counsel. In deciding whether to talk to defense counsel, the professional should consult with the child if the child is mature enough to assist in decision making. Additionally, parents or caretakers should be consulted. A word of caution is appropriate. If the professional decides against speaking with defense counsel prior to trial, it should come as no surprise at trial when the defense attorney asks, "I called you about this case prior to trial, but you refused even to talk to me, didn't you?" The purpose of this question, of course, is to give the jury the impression that the professional is not objective. Following such a question, the professional may provide an explanation for the decision not to communicate with defense counsel. (See Chapter 3 for discussion of subpoenas.)

The professional should consider whether discussing the case with the defense might inadvertently reveal information about the child that is protected from disclosure by a privilege such as the psychotherapist-client privilege, or by the ethical obligation of professionals to safeguard the confidences and secrets of clients. (See Chapter 3 for discussion of confidentiality and privilege.)

There are many times when it is appropriate, and in the child's best interest, for the professional to communicate with defense counsel. For example, following consultation with the treating therapist, the defendant's attorney may be persuaded that the best course is for the defendant to plead guilty and seek treatment as an alternative to prison. This alternative spares the child the ordeal of testifying in court.

When considering whether or not to communicate with defense counsel, professionals should proceed with caution, and should keep in mind that the defense attorney has *one* responsibility—to provide zealous representation for the accused. Many defense attorneys are sensitive to the child's welfare, but the defense attorney does *not* represent the child, and if the child's needs conflict with the rights of the accused, defense counsel is ethically bound to protect the defendant, even at the expense of the child.

Before communicating with defense counsel, the professional might contact the prosecutor assigned to the case. Prosecutors are not supposed to discourage witnesses from talking to the defense. The prosecutor may, however, give advice about the consequences of communicating with defense counsel.

If the professional is acquainted with an attorney in private law practice, a quick telephone call can dispel doubts about talking to defense counsel. Professionals employed by government agencies consult with supervisors before discussing cases with representatives of the defense.

Most professionals working with children feel more comfortable discussing a case with the prosecutor than with defense counsel. But here, too, a degree of forethought is advisable. Generally, professionals who treat children are not at liberty to disclose confidential information to the prosecutor without permission from someone in a position to authorize disclosure.

Prosecutors generally are sensitive to the welfare of child victims. Indeed, many prosecutors view the child as their second client—the first client being the citizens of the community. Nevertheless, the prosecutor in a criminal case is not the child's attorney, and cases arise in which the prosecutor's strategic decisions are not in the child's best interest. Thus, although professionals working with abused and neglected children are usually justified in the ease with which they interact with prosecutors, it is advisable, especially for professionals treating children, to maintain a degree of professional distance from both sides of the adversarial struggle. Naturally, when a professional is retained to testify as an expert witness for the prosecution or the defense, a close working relationship with the attorney is necessary and appropriate.

Professionals who provide treatment for individuals accused of child abuse are careful to protect confidential information about their clients. When the professional is contacted by the defense attorney or the prosecutor, the advice outlined above is, for the most part, applicable. The client should be consulted about communication with attorneys and the release of confidential information.

As part of trial preparation, the defense attorney may seek to interview the child. Is the child required to submit to an interview with defense counsel? If so, does the interview occur in the defense attorney's office, or in some more neutral location? Finally, does the defendant have a right to attend the interview? These are difficult questions. On the one hand, the child is often the prosecution's most important witness, and the defense attorney's ability to prepare for trial may be handicapped if he or she is not permitted to interview the child. Exclusion of the defendant from a pretrial interview may interfere with the ability of the defense attorney to ask the most effective questions. On the other hand, an interview by the defendant's attorney may be difficult for the child, and seeing the defendant may be quite traumatic. In some states, the judge in charge of the case has authority to permit the defense to interview the child prior to trial. The judge may impose conditions on the interview to ensure that the child is not harassed or traumatized. In quite a few states, an adult responsible for the child may refuse to allow the child to be interviewed prior to trial (Myers, 1992).

THE TRIAL

Only a small percentage of criminal cases proceed all the way to trial. In felony cases the defendant has the right to a jury trial. The defendant can waive the right to a jury, and when this occurs, the judge functions as both judge and jury. Cases tried before the judge alone are called bench trials.

Jury Selection

The first step in a jury trial is to select a jury from a panel of prospective jurors. The panel is sometimes called a *venire*, and the prospective jurors are referred to as *veniremen* or *venirewomen*. During jury selection, prospective jurors are asked questions to determine their ability to reach an impartial decision. The questioning process is called *voir dire*, and in many states the lawyers do the questioning. In other states, and in the federal courts, the judge asks the questions.

Prospective jurors can be excused from the panel by the judge. If a prospective juror's answers to questions indicate inability to act impartially, one of the attorneys may ask the judge to excuse the juror from the panel. If the judge agrees with the attorney, the judge excuses the individual for cause. The prosecutor and defense attorney may ask that any number of prospective jurors be excused for cause.

A second method to excuse prospective jurors is for one of the attorneys to use a peremptory challenge. Each attorney is allowed a small number of peremptory challenges. Generally, attorneys do not have to explain or justify a decision to excuse a prospective juror through peremptory challenge, and attorneys rely on their common sense and experience. For example, a defense attorney might use a peremptory challenge to prevent a police officer from serving on the jury. Another peremptory challenge might be used to exclude a parent whose child was sexually abused. Assuming that both the police officer and the parent stated they could be impartial, neither could be excused for cause, and defense counsel would have to use two peremptory challenges. When jury selection is complete, the jury is empaneled.

Opening Statements

The next step in the trial is the opening statements by the attorneys. The prosecutor goes first, and explains to the jury what he or she believes the evidence will show. Following this, it is the defense attorney's turn to inform the jury of the defendant's perspective on the case. The opening statements of the attorneys are not evidence. Indeed, nothing an attorney says during trial is officially evidence unless the attorney testifies as a witness. Needless to say, although the statements and questions of the lawyers are not evidence, everyone knows that what the attorneys say can have an impact on the jury.

Presentation of Evidence

With opening statements complete, the prosecutor begins presenting evidence of the defendant's guilt. *Evidence* has been defined as "any matter, verbal or physical, that can be used to support the existence of a factual proposition" (Lilly, 1987, p. 2). Thus evidence includes testimony of witnesses, written documents, and objects. Any evidence that helps prove a disputed issue is admissible unless some rule excludes the evidence (*Federal Rules of Evidence*, 402).

The prosecutor's presentation of evidence is called the state's case-in-chief. The most important evidence against the defendant is usually the testimony of witnesses, including the child, and, in selected cases, expert witnesses. There is one person the prosecutor cannot call as a witness, and that is the defendant. A person accused of crime has a constitutional right to refuse to testify, and the prosecutor can neither call the defendant as a witness nor comment to the jury on the defendant's decision not to testify.

An individual testifying as a witness takes an oath to testify truthfully. Once the oath is administered, the attorney who called the witness begins asking questions. Questioning by the attorney who called the witness is called direct examination. Following direct examination, the opposing attorney may cross-examine the witness.

When a child testifies for the prosecution during the state's case-in-chief, the defense attorney usually cross-examines the child. Frequently, the goal of cross-examination is to attack the child's credibility. For example, defense counsel may focus cross-examination on the fact that the child delayed reporting the abuse for many months, and recanted following disclosure. Defense counsel will attempt to convince the jury that the delay and recantation indicate that abuse never occurred, and that the child is lying or has been coached. When the defense seeks to undermine the child's credibility, the judge may permit the prosecutor to offer what is called rebuttal evidence. Rebuttal evidence is often provided by expert witnesses, and is designed to inform jurors that delay in reporting and recantation are common in sexually abused children. (See Chapter 5 for discussion of expert testimony.)

When the prosecutor completes the presentation of evidence, the prosecution rests its case. Defense counsel then begins the defense case-in-chief. In many cases, the accused person takes the witness stand during the defense case-in-chief and denies the abuse. Testifying is always a calculated risk for a defendant. Although the prosecutor cannot call the defendant as a witness, once the defendant testifies, the prosecutor has the right to cross-examine him or her, and the prosecutor's cross-examination may cast the defendant in an unfavorable light with the jury. Thus, to avoid the possibility of damaging cross-examination by the prosecutor, the defendant may decide not to testify. When the defense has presented its evidence, the defense rests.

After the defense rests its case, the prosecutor may offer rebuttal evidence. This portion of the trial is called the state's case-in-rebuttal. Expert witnesses sometimes testify during rebuttal.

Closing Arguments

When all the evidence has been submitted, and the prosecution and defense have rested, the attorneys present closing arguments to the jury. The prosecutor goes first, followed by defense counsel. When defense counsel finishes, the prosecutor has the final opportunity to address the jury. During closing argument, an attorney is permitted to urge jurors to interpret the evidence in a way that favors the attorney's client. In addition, the attorney is allowed to argue that the jurors should believe certain witness and disbelieve others. Thus the prosecutor could say, "Now, ladies and gentlemen,

I'm going to tell you why you should disbelieve the defendant and reject his testimony." The prosecutor then reviews the weaknesses in the defendant's testimony. Naturally, the defense attorney has the same right, and during defense counsel's closing argument in a child abuse case the attorney might say, "Ladies and gentlemen, you should not believe the child's testimony. Why? Because she told no one about the alleged abuse for more than a year, and because she had a strong motive to fabricate the allegations." Closing arguments can be dramatic, and fictionalized trials on television and in the movies often exploit this part of the trial process.

Jury Deliberation—Appeal

Following closing arguments by the attorneys, the judge instructs the jury on the law that the jury must use to decide whether the defendant is guilty. The jury then retires to the jury room to deliberate and reach a verdict. If the jury returns a verdict of not guilty, the case is over. The prosecution cannot appeal a verdict of acquittal. If the jury convicts, however, the defendant has the right to appeal the conviction to the appropriate appellate court. The appellate court judges consider all the evidence presented at trial, including a verbatim transcript of the testimony. The appellate judges study the legal briefs submitted by the attorneys, and, in most cases, the attorneys present oral argument before the appellate court.

The appellate court determines whether mistakes were made during the trial that are sufficiently serious to warrant a new trial for the defendant. If no serious errors occurred during the trial, the appellate court affirms the conviction. If errors occurred that substantially affected the defendant's right to a fair trial, the appellate court reverses the conviction. When a conviction is reversed on appeal, the prosecutor usually has the option to put the defendant through a second trial. In child abuse cases, a second trial usually means, of course, that the child must testify again.

Roger Redding's Case

Roger Redding's case was tried before a jury. Vickie testified against her father, although testifying was very difficult. Like so many incest victims, Vickie was torn between love for her dad and her desire to stop the abuse. Vickie's sister, Ruth, testified, and described how she too had been molested by Roger. The arresting officer testified and repeated for the jury Roger's incriminating statements at the time of his arrest. The pediatrician testified, and described the medical evidence of sexual abuse. The doctor also repeated for the jury Vickie's description of her abuse at the time of the initial visit to the doctor's office.

Roger's attorney vigorously cross-examined Vickie in an effort to undermine her credibility in the eyes of the jury. The attorney focused many questions on the fact that Vickie waited a long time to reveal her abuse. Ruth was also cross-examined about why she kept her alleged molestation secret so long. Essentially, defense counsel attempted to persuade the jury the girls were lying. Following the attack on Vickie and Ruth's credibility, the prosecutor called an expert witness who explained to the jury that many sexually abused children delay reporting.

Roger testified in his own behalf, and denied that he touched his children in a sexual way. Roger testified that the girls were coached into false allegations by their psychotherapist.

The jury deliberated for two days, and still could not reach a decision. The hours dragged like years as everyone waited on pins and needles. Finally, on the third day of deliberations, the jury informed the judge that it had reached a verdict. Everyone rushed back to the courtroom. Roger sat stony faced and pale next to his attorney. Roger's wife, Beth, sat in the public area of the courtroom wringing her hands. Vickie and Ruth were at their grandmother's home, anxiously awaiting news of their father's fate. The judge turned to the jury and said, "Ladies and gentlemen of the jury, have you reached a verdict?" The foreman stood and replied, "Yes we have, your honor." The judge said, "What is your verdict?" The foreman nervously fingered the slip of paper clenched in his hand. Slowly, the foreman opened the paper and read the words, "We find Roger Redding guilty." Roger put his head down on the table, and his attorney put a consoling arm on his shoulder. Beth sobbed quietly. When Beth telephoned the news to Vickie and Ruth, the girls wept in a confusion of grief and relief.

SENTENCING

When a person pleads guilty or is found guilty following a trial, the judge imposes sentence. States have complicated rules governing sentencing. Depending on the crime involved and the history and circumstances of the defendant, the judge may sentence the defendant to a term of imprisonment. In some cases, the defendant receives a prison sentence but the judge suspends the prison term and places the individual on probation under the supervision of the probation department. In child sexual abuse cases, some defendants are allowed probation on condition they receive treatment for their deviancy. Failure to attend or participate meaningfully in treatment constitutes a violation of probation, and the judge may reinstate the prison term provided in the original sentence.

In Roger Redding's case, the judge sentenced Roger to five years in state prison. All but six months of the sentence was suspended. Roger served six months in the county jail, and was then placed on probation. As a condition of his probation, Roger was required to move out of the family home. He was to have no contact with his children until he completed a rigorous course of treatment, and his therapist recommended gradual family reunification. At last report, Roger was participating in therapy. Vickie and Ruth were also in therapy, and were recovering. Somehow, Beth found the courage to bring her children through this difficult experience. She has not decided what the future holds for her marriage with Roger. For now, Beth is satisfied with helping her children heal.

❏ Overview of the Legal System

Law is the social institution through which society provides order and protection for its members. Two sources of power underlie the legal system: the police power and the *parens patriae* authority. The police power authorizes the government to prevent people from harming one another. State legislators rely on the police power when they enact statutes prohibiting child abuse and neglect. Law enforcement officers and CPS professionals rely on the police power when they take abused and neglected children into emergency protective custody.

The police power is supplemented by the *parens patriae* authority, under which the state has limited power to protect people, including children, who cannot protect themselves. The Latin term *parens patriae* comes from English law. The English king was *parens patriae*, or father of his country, and had authority to protect children within the realm. When the United States gained independence from England, the *parens patriae* authority was vested in state legislatures. Through the combined authority of the police and *parens patriae* powers, states have ample authority to protect abused and neglected children.

THE STATE'S INTEREST IN CHILD WELFARE

The government has a long-standing interest in the welfare of children. The U.S. Supreme Court described this interest in *Prince v. Massachusetts* (1944), where the Court wrote that "the state's assertion of authority to [protect children] is no mere corporate concern of official authority. It is the interest of youth itself, that children be both safeguarded from abuses and given opportunities for growth into free and independent citizens." The state's interest is particularly compelling in the context of child abuse. The Supreme Court has characterized the state's interest in protecting children as an "objective of surpassing importance" (*New York v. Ferber*, 1982, p. 757).

UNITED STATES AND STATE CONSTITUTIONS

The U.S. Constitution is the fundamental source of law in the United States. It establishes the federal government and distinguishes the federal government from state governments. The U.S. Constitution divides the federal government into three branches: the legislative branch, Congress; the executive branch, headed by the President; and the judicial branch, or the federal courts. The Bill of Rights consists of amendments to the original Constitution. The U.S. Supreme Court has ruled that the Bill of Rights extends important rights to parents, children, and families. For example, parents have a constitutional right to freedom from unwarranted government intrusion into the privacy of the family.

Every state has its own constitution and bill of rights. Like the U.S. Constitution, state constitutions create three branches of government: the state legislature; the executive branch, led by the governor; and the state court system. State bills of rights are generally very similar to the federal Bill of Rights, although some state constitutions contain rights that are not found in the U.S. Constitution.

If a state legislature passes a law that is inconsistent with the U.S. Constitution or a federal statute enacted by Congress, the U.S. Constitution or the federal statute prevails. Within the sphere of its authority, federal constitutional and statutory law is supreme, and takes precedence over conflicting state laws.

FEDERAL AND STATE STATUTES
RELATING TO CHILD ABUSE AND NEGLECT

Laws relating to child abuse and neglect come from three sources: statutes, regulations promulgated by agencies of the executive branch of government, and court decisions. On the federal level, Congress has enacted several laws that affect child protection efforts. In 1974, Congress passed the Child Abuse Prevention and Treatment Act, which created the National Center on Child Abuse and Neglect. Among other things, the National Center provides federal funding for research "into the causes of child abuse and neglect, and into the prevention, identification, and treatment thereof" (United States Code Annotated, Title 42, § 5101[b][5]). Another important federal statute is the Adoption Assistance and Child Welfare Act of 1980, commonly known as Public Law 96-272, which requires states to make reasonable efforts to prevent removal of maltreated children from parental custody. Congress also enacted legislation relating to Native American children (United States Code Annotated, Title 25, § 1901). Among other things, the federal Indian Child Welfare Act requires agencies to make "active efforts" to provide services "designed to prevent the breakup of the Indian family."

State legislatures are constantly at work on legislation relating to child abuse and neglect. State criminal codes define child abuse and neglect and establish punishments. Reporting laws exist in every state. State statutes create CPS agencies, juvenile courts, and other social agencies, and charge them with herculean responsibilities.

REGULATIONS

Enacting statutes is the exclusive province of the legislature. Professionals working with abused and neglected children know, however, that statutes are not the only laws affecting practice. Agencies of the executive branch of government have authority to promulgate administrative regulations. Federal administrative regulations are compiled in the Code of Federal Regulations, which consists of 200 volumes! State administrative regulations are contained in state administrative codes. Administrative regulations have the same force of law as statutes enacted by the legislature.

An example may help illustrate the complex web of federal and state statutes and regulations that govern many programs for children. In 1975, Congress enacted the Education for All Handicapped Children Act (Public Law 94-142) to provide handicapped children with appropriate educational opportunities. Congress charged the U.S. Department of Education with administering the act. In its turn, the department promulgated regulations to implement the act. As is often the case, the agency regulations actually have a more important impact on day-to-day practice than the statute itself. The layers of law do not end with the federal statute and its implementing regulations, however, because states promulgate their own statutes and administrative regulations regarding special education. And that's not all! Added to the labyrinth of federal and state statutes and regulations are mountains of agency policies, protocols, and procedures. Sometimes it takes a lawyer just to *find* the applicable law, let alone understand it.

COMMON LAW

Although much of the law affecting practice with abused and neglected children takes the form of statutes and regulations, another important source of law requires mention. Appellate courts have limited authority to create law. Law created by judicial decision is called common law. Decisions of the U.S. Supreme Court and state appellate courts create legally binding precedents, some of which are very important for professionals working with children. For example, in *Maryland v. Craig* (1990), the U.S. Supreme Court ruled that certain traumatized children may testify without having to face the person accused of sexually abusing them. The Supreme Court's *Craig* decision gives prosecutors across the United States the green light to use state statutes that permit selected children to avoid the trauma of face-to-face confrontation with their abusers.

2

Legal Implications of Interviewing Children Who May Be Abused or Neglected

Interviewing children about possible abuse or neglect is a difficult task, requiring skill, patience, and flexibility. This chapter discusses the increasingly important legal implications that arise when children are interviewed. Because the legal implications are at their height in the context of sexual abuse, that is the focus of this chapter.

The emphasis here is on interviews that are conducted to determine whether or not a child has been sexually abused. Thus this chapter is pertinent for CPS, law enforcement, mental health, and medical professionals conducting investigative interviews. It is also relevant for medical and mental health professionals who interview children to determine whether treatment is necessary for the effects of sexual abuse. The legal implications are similar whether the interviewer's goals are investigative or therapeutic.

❏   The Attack on the Interviewer

During the 1980s, when charges of child sexual abuse were filed against an individual, who was the primary target of the defense attorney? The child. The defense often asserted that young children are incompetent witnesses. Defense counsel argued that children have poor memories, cannot differentiate fact from fantasy, and do not understand the need to tell the truth. The attack on older children and adolescents sometimes centered on charges that these children were seeking revenge.

The child is often the state's most important witness, and it is not improper for the defense to undermine the child's credibility. Such efforts by the defense will continue. Some children are not competent to testify, and an occasional child lies or distorts the truth. What is troubling today, however, in the 1990s, is a change in emphasis in the defense of child sexual abuse charges. Increasingly, defense counsel takes aim not at the child, but at the professionals who interviewed or treated the child.

Until recently, professionals were seldom the target of defense efforts to prove that sexual abuse did not occur, but that has changed. The new rallying cry of the defense is, Attack the interviewer. The charge is made that interviewers ask leading questions. Interviewers coerce malleable young minds into believing they were involved in events that never occurred. Interviewers lack objectivity. Professionals are zealots on a witch-hunt. The bottom line of this defense strategy is that children interviewed by professionals cannot be believed.

The new rallying cry of the defense is, Attack the interviewer.

What evidence is there of growing distrust of professionals who interview children? The most pertinent source of evidence is the increasing number of court decisions in which the way children are interviewed has been a central issue (*Idaho v. Wright*, 1990). The attack on the interviewer takes place outside the courtroom also. Raskin and Yuille (1989) warn "of the problematic nature of interviews of children as they are currently conducted. . . . Inadequacies in such methods frequently lead to lack of substantiation of valid allegations and may also reinforce false allegations of sexual abuse" (p. 184).

Improper interview techniques are fair game for criticism, and defense attorneys and their expert witnesses act responsibly when they challenge such techniques. Sometimes, however, the attack on the interviewer goes too far. *Harper's Magazine* published an article comparing child protection efforts to the Salem witchcraft trials (Rabinowitz, 1990). Wakefield and Underwager (1988) assert that *most* of what children say during interviews is untrustworthy, claiming that the "procedures followed in the typical interrogation of children contaminate, confuse, and make statements made by children unreliable" (p. 33).[1]

Criticism of interview practices ranges from legitimate to illegitimate, from temperate to outlandish. There is unquestionably much to criticize in the way some children are interviewed. Criticism that is legitimate and constructive is difficult to hear, but it needs to be heard. One wonders, however, what the uninformed public must think when they read in the popular media that professionals who talk to children are the modern-day equivalent of the Grand Inquisitor. Clearly, the professional community must get its house in order so that interviewing practices can be defended against the growing onslaught of criticism. As part of this housecleaning, this chapter analyzes the important legal implications of professional interviews of children who may have been sexually abused. Whether we like it or not, important legal implications arise whenever children are questioned regarding abuse.

There are both positive and negative legal implications of interviews. On the positive side, interviews provide unique opportunities to gather evidence of child abuse. On the negative side, an interview that is poorly conducted from the legal perspective can cripple the ability to protect a child from further abuse.

❑ Interviews as Opportunities to Gather Evidence of Child Abuse and Neglect

The overriding goal of the interview is to find out whether or not abuse occurred. The child's statements are the gateway to this goal. Relatively few professionals realize, however, that the legal implications of the interview extend *far* beyond disclosure. Interviews provide unique opportunities to document the often fleeting evidence that is essential to prove sexual abuse. The U.S. Supreme Court has observed that "child abuse is one of the most difficult crimes to detect and prosecute" (*Pennsylvania v. Ritchie,* 1987, p. 60). Physical and medical evidence exists in only a minority of cases (Myers et al., 1989). Seldom are there eyewitnesses to abuse. Although some children are excellent witnesses, others are too frightened or too young to take the witness stand and describe what happened to them. Thus in many cases the critical legal issue is whether enough evidence can be gathered to protect the child.

HEARSAY

Interviews are gold mines of evidence that can be used in legal proceedings. But if the interviewer does not know what to watch for and document, the opportunity to preserve this evidence is lost. And the important evidence that is lost most frequently is that of the child's own statements about sexual abuse. Much of what children say—and some of what they do—during interviews is considered hearsay. Although hearsay is generally not allowed in court, there are exceptions to the rule against hearsay. Children's hearsay statements play an exceedingly important role in child abuse litigation, and interviewers hold the key to increasing the likelihood that children's hearsay statements can be used in court.

The intricacies of hearsay are among the most complex in the law. Indeed, many lawyers have only a tenuous grasp of the subject. Interviewers may say, "Well, how can *I* be expected to understand hearsay if the lawyers can't figure it out half the time?!" Fortunately, it is not necessary to master the nuances of hearsay to deal effectively with its implications for practice. It is helpful, however, to have an introductory understanding of hearsay. The following definition provides a starting place.

A child's words are hearsay if

1. the child's words were intended by the child to describe something that happened;

   and

2. the child's words were spoken prior to the court proceeding at which the words are repeated by someone who heard the child speak;

   and

3. the child's words are offered in court to prove that what the child said actually happened.

The best way to unravel hearsay is through examples. Consider the case of 4-year-old Sally Jones, who was allegedly molested by a neighbor. Immediately upon her release by the offender, Sally ran crying to her mother and said, "Mommy, mommy, Bill played nasty with me. He put his finger in my pee-pee!" Bill is charged with molestation, which he denies. There is no medical or physical evidence of abuse.

At Bill's trial, Sally does not testify because she is too frightened to communicate.[2] The prosecutor has a dilemma. How can the prosecutor prove sexual abuse when the only eyewitness cannot testify? One way is to call Sally's mother, Mrs. Jones, as a witness, and ask Mrs. Jones to repeat Sally's description of Bill's conduct. That is, the prosecutor uses what Sally said *to her mother* as proof that Sally was abused.

Mrs. Jones takes the witness stand. The prosecutor asks some preliminary questions, and then comes to the point, "Mrs. Jones, what did Sally say to you when she ran into the house that day?" But before Sally's mother can repeat what her daughter said, the defense attorney interrupts and says, "Your honor, I object. The prosecutor's question calls for hearsay." Is defense counsel right? Should the judge sustain the objection and prohibit Mrs. Jones from repeating Sally's description because Sally's words are hearsay? To answer this question, consider the definition of hearsay.

Sally intended her words ("Mommy, mommy, Bill played nasty with me. He put his finger in my pee-pee!") to describe something that happened to her. Thus the first element of the hearsay definition is satisfied. (In discussing hearsay, the words spoken by the child are usually referred to as a *statement*.)

Sally's statement describing her abuse was made prior to Bill's trial, and, at the trial, Sally's mother proposes to repeat what her daughter said. Thus the second element of hearsay is satisfied.

Finally, the prosecutor is offering Sally's statement to prove that what Sally said actually happened, that is, to prove that what Sally said is true. All three elements of the definition are satisfied, and Sally's statement is hearsay. Unless the prosecutor can think of some way around the general rule against using hearsay in court, the judge will sustain defense counsel's objection, and Sally's mother will not be permitted to repeat Sally's description of her abuse.

As a second example, suppose Sally was taken to a hospital shortly after her initial disclosure to her mother. At the hospital, Sally was interviewed by a social worker. The interview with the social worker took place half an hour after Sally disclosed her abuse to her mother. Sally had stopped crying, but she was still visibly upset. In response to the social worker's questions about what happened, Sally pointed to her genital area and said, "Bill put his finger in me and it hurt a lot." The social worker then handed Sally an anatomical diagram and asked Sally to circle the part of the diagram where she was touched. Sally circled the genital area. Finally, the social worker handed Sally anatomical dolls and asked her to illustrate what happened. Sally said the adult doll was Bill, and the child doll was her. Sally placed the adult doll's hand on the genital area of the child doll and pushed.

At Bill's trial, the prosecutor calls the social worker as a witness, and asks the social worker to repeat Sally's description of what Bill did, including Sally's gesture pointing to her genital area. The prosecutor also asks the social worker to describe what Sally did with the anatomical diagram and dolls. Once again, however, defense counsel says, "Your honor, I object. This question too calls for hearsay."

When Sally spoke to the social worker, Sally intended to describe what Bill did to her. Thus Sally's words satisfy the first element of the hearsay definition. But that's not all. When Sally pointed to her genital area, she was also describing something that happened to her. The same is true of Sally's drawing on the diagram and her positioning of the anatomical dolls. Sally used nonverbal communication to describe something that happened.

Is Sally's nonverbal communication hearsay? Nonverbal communication that is intended to describe something that happened can be hearsay. Consider a simple example. Suppose that shortly following her abuse, Sally is taken to the police station to see whether she can pick her assailant out of a lineup. Seven men walk onto the stage, and the police officer says, "Now Sally, do you see the man who hurt you?" Sally could say, "Yes, that's him. Right in the middle." Alternatively, Sally might say nothing, and point to the man in the middle. The message is the same whether Sally uses words or a gesture. Sally's pointing gesture is the equivalent of words. Like the words, "That's him," Sally's gesture is hearsay if the police officer testifies at Bill's trial and describes Sally's pointing gesture at the line up.

The words Sally spoke to the social worker, along with Sally's nonverbal communication, occurred prior to the court proceeding at which they are used as evidence, therefore the second element of the hearsay definition is satisfied.

Finally, if the prosecutor uses Sally's verbal and nonverbal communication with the social worker to prove that Sally was abused as Sally described, then the final element of the hearsay definition is satisfied. Unless the prosecutor can somehow circumvent the hearsay rule, the judge will prohibit the social worker from describing what Sally said and did during the interview.

Escape Hatches From
the Definition of Hearsay

Recall that a child's words are hearsay *only* when the child intends to describe something that happened *and* when the child's words are used in court to prove that what the child said is true. With the elements of hearsay in mind, it is possible to fashion two escape hatches from hearsay. First, a child's words are hearsay *only* if the words were intended by the child to describe something that happened. Second, a child's words are hearsay only when they are used to prove exactly what the child said.[3]

Turning to the first escape hatch from hearsay, a child's words are hearsay only if the child intended to describe something that happened. When a child speaks or acts without the intent to describe something that happened, the first element of the hearsay definition is missing, and the child's words or conduct are not hearsay. Suppose, for example, that during Sally's interview at the hospital, the social worker mentioned Bill's name. At the mention of the name, Sally began trembling. She ran to her mother and hid her face in her skirt, sobbing, "Mommy, mommy." Sally's conduct and words were not intended by her as descriptions of events, and are not hearsay (*In re Penelope B.*, 1985).

As another example, consider a 4-year-old's interaction with anatomical dolls. Without prompting, the child places the penis of one doll in the mouth of another doll and says, "Suck me." The child's conduct and words are indicative of abuse. If the child intended to describe something that happened to her or to another child, then her interaction with the dolls is hearsay. But if the child did not intend to describe something that happened, then her behavior is not hearsay. The outcome depends on the child's subjective state of mind at the time.

When a child says or does something during an interview without intending to describe an event, it may be possible to use the child's words or acts in court without affront to the rule against hearsay. Interviews can be structured to increase the likelihood that children engage in verbal and nonverbal behavior that is not intended to describe events. For example, prior to questioning about abuse, a young child might be allowed a period of free play. Some aspects of the child's nondirected play with dolls, drawing materials, and other toys may provide evidence of abuse. Yet, if the child's play is not intended by the child as a description of events, it may not be hearsay. The interviewer might leave the room to reduce the likelihood that play is intended as a description of events directed to the interviewer. The child's behavior can be observed through a one-way mirror.

The second escape hatch from the definition of hearsay involves use of words that *were* intended by the child to describe an event.

Rather than the words being used to prove the event, however, the words are used to prove something else. For example, suppose a 4-year-old is being interviewed. The child says, "Daddy's pee-pee was big and hard, like a stick, and it hurt when he pushed it in my mouth, and white glue came out that tasted really yucky." What powerful evidence of sexual abuse! Yet, if the child's words are used in court to prove the literal truth of what the child said, that is, that the child's father had an erection and ejaculated in the child's mouth, then the words are hearsay. Unless the child's words satisfy the requirements of one of the hearsay exceptions discussed below, the jury will not hear this compelling evidence of sexual abuse. Fortunately, the child's words need not be used to prove the literal truth of what the child said. Instead, the child's statement may be used to prove that the child possessed developmentally unusual knowledge of sexual acts and anatomy. Used to prove developmentally unusual sexual knowledge, the child's words are not hearsay! Why? Because the words are not used to prove the literal content of what the child said. By escaping the definition of hearsay, the prosecutor increases the odds the jury will hear the child's graphic description of abuse.

The ability to protect children through the legal system sometimes turns on the capacity of the prosecutor to convince the judge that a child's words are not hearsay. Unless the professionals who interviewed the child knew to document what happened during the interview, however, the prosecutor will not have the information required to persuade the judge that one of the escape hatches from hearsay applies.

There are many times when it is not possible to escape the hearsay definition. Furthermore, there are many occasions when the prosecutor wants to use a child's statement to prove precisely what the child said. The prosecutor acknowledges that the statement is hearsay, but seeks to use the statement in court anyway. Is this possible? Yes, it is possible in some cases because there are exceptions to the general rule against using hearsay in court. Interviewers play an immensely important role in documenting the often fleeting information that the prosecutor *must* know if he or she is to convince a judge that a child's hearsay statement meets the requirements of one of the hearsay exceptions. Unfortunately, too few interviewers know

Table 2.1 Elements of the Excited Utterance Exception

1. The child experiences a startling event.
2. The child makes a statement relating to the startling event.
3. The child's statement is made while the child is still experiencing the excitement caused by the startling event.

what to watch for and document, and, as a consequence, children's hearsay statements that fit beautifully into hearsay exceptions are regularly lost as evidence.

Hearsay Exceptions

Exceptions to the rule against using hearsay in court are created for categories of hearsay statements that are considered reliable. Although there are many hearsay exceptions, only a few play a day-to-day role in child abuse and neglect litigation.

The excited utterance exception. An excited utterance is a hearsay statement that relates to a startling event. The statement must be made while the child is still under the excitement caused by the startling event. Excited utterances can be used in court even though they are hearsay. Three requirements must be fulfilled for a child's hearsay statement to be an excited utterance.

First, the child must experience a startling event that excites the child. Recall Sally's case, in which Sally was molested by the neighbor, Bill. The molestation qualifies as a startling event. Not all acts of sexual abuse startle or excite children, but Sally's experience was sufficiently startling for the excited utterance exception.

Second, the child's statement must relate to the startling event. Sally's statement to her mother described the abuse, and clearly meets the relationship requirement. The statement to the social worker also referred directly to the event, and meets the relationship requirement.

Finally, the child's hearsay statement must be made while the child is still experiencing the excitement caused by the startling event. Sally reported the abuse to her mother shortly after it occurred, and while she was still upset and crying. Thus Sally's statement to her mother is an excited utterance and can be used in court even though it is hearsay. The judge will overrule defense counsel's objection, and Sally's mother will be permitted to tell the jury what her daughter said that day. But what about the statement to the social worker? Is Sally's statement to the social worker, at least half an hour after the sexual abuse, and in response to the social worker's questions, an excited utterance?

Judges consider all relevant circumstances to determine whether a hearsay statement is an excited utterance. Interviewers can watch for and document the following important factors:

Nature of the event. Certain events are more startling than others. Judges consider the nature of the event, and the likely effect such an event would have on a child of similar age and experience.

Lapse of time. The longer the delay between a startling event and a child's hearsay statement describing the event, the less likely the child was still excited when the statement was made. Judges agree, however, that lapse of time is not dispositive on the issue of excitement, and delay is considered along with other factors indicating presence or absence of excitement. Judges have approved delays ranging from a few minutes to many hours.

Emotional condition. A child's emotional condition is an important indicator of excitement. If a child was upset and crying when a statement was made, the judge is more likely to conclude that the statement is an excited utterance. On the other hand, if the child was calm when the statement was made, or if a period of calm or sleep intervened between a startling event and a child's statement relating to the event, the statement is less likely to qualify as an excited utterance.

Speech pattern. The way a child makes a statement may indicate excitement. For example, pressured or hurried speech indicates excitement. Sally's statement to her mother is an illustration. Sally said, "Mommy, mommy, Bill played nasty with me. He put his finger in my

Table 2.2 Factors Indicating Whether Child Is Still Experiencing the Excitement Caused by the Startling Event

- nature of the event
- lapse of time
- child's emotional condition
- speech pattern
- words spoken
- child's physical condition
- spontaneity
- questioning by adults
- statement made at first safe opportunity

pee-pee!" The fact that the sentence ends in an exclamation point indicates excitement.

Words spoken. The child's words themselves may indicate excitement.

Physical condition. A child's physical condition may indicate whether the child is excited. For example, statements from a child who is injured or in pain are more likely to qualify as excited utterances.

Spontaneity. In evaluating a statement as a potential excited utterance, the most important factor is whether the statement is a product of reflection and deliberation or a spontaneous response to a startling event. The more spontaneous the statement, the more likely it is to meet the requirements of this hearsay exception.

Questioning. A child may make a statement in response to questioning by an adult. The way a child is questioned has an impact on whether a statement is an excited utterance. Judges agree that questioning does not necessarily destroy the spontaneity required by the exception. When questioning is leading, however, spontaneity may be lacking (leading questions will be discussed later in this chapter).

First safe opportunity. Most children are abused while under the exclusive control of the abuser. When the child is finally released, and is in a safe environment where the child is able to disclose what happened, a substantial period of time may have elapsed, raising questions about whether the child's statement is an excited utterance. Several court decisions state that when a child makes a hearsay statement at the first safe opportunity, the statement may qualify as an excited utterance (Myers, 1992).

Returning now to Sally's hearsay statement to the social worker, half an hour after the initial disclosure, and in response to the social worker's questions: Is Sally's statement an excited utterance? This is a close case. One thing is certain, however. Unless the social worker documented the factors described above, and carefully preserved Sally's words, there is little chance the judge will conclude that Sally's statement to the social worker was an excited utterance. In the final analysis, the ability to use Sally's words as evidence that she was abused depends less on the skill of the prosecutor than on the documentation of the social worker.

Fresh complaint of rape. Under a venerable legal doctrine called "fresh complaint of rape," an adult rape victim's initial disclosure can be used in court to corroborate the victim's testimony (Myers, 1992). The fresh complaint doctrine applies to children as well as adults,[4] and is not limited to rape cases. Thus, regardless of the type of sex offense, a child's fresh complaint regarding the offense may be admissible.

A child's description of sexual abuse that does not qualify as an excited utterance—perhaps because the time lapse is too great— may be used in court as a fresh complaint.[5] A child's disclosure of abuse may qualify as a fresh complaint even though it is made weeks or months following the abuse.

The exception for hearsay statements describing a child's emotions, beliefs, or physical condition. One of the most theoretically complex exceptions to the rule against hearsay is the exception that allows limited use in court of statements describing a person's emotions, sensations, or physical condition. Among the many states of mind allowed under this exception are statements indicating intent, plan, motive, pain, love, and hate. This book is not the place to work through the complexities of the "state of mind" exception. For present purposes, suffice it to say that interviewers can assist attorneys by documenting statements that describe children's emotions, including feelings of affection, fear, and dislike. Additionally, interviewers should document state- ments describing bodily feeling. Finally, interviewers should docu- ment the child's belief that abuse occurred.

Statements made to professionals providing diagnosis and/or treatment for the child. Most states have an exception to the hearsay rule for certain statements made to professionals providing treatment or diagnostic services for children.[6] This exception, commonly called the medical diagnosis or treatment exception, includes the child's statements describing medical history. The medical history "consists of data identifying the patient, the source of referral to the doctor, the name of the person providing the medical history, and chief complaint, a history of the present illness, past medical history, family history, psychosocial history, and a review of body systems" (Myers et al., 1989, p. 36). Also included in the medical diagnosis or treatment exception are statements describing the child's past and present symptoms, pain, and other sensations. Finally, the exception allows use in court of the child's description of the cause of injury or illness.

The primary rationale for the diagnosis or treatment exception is that hearsay statements made to professionals providing diagnostic or treatment services are reliable. Reliability exists because individuals have a strong incentive to be truthful with health care providers (Mosteller, 1989). After all, a person's health—even life—may depend on the accuracy of information he or she provides to a physician or nurse. This rationale is applicable for many older children and adolescents. Young children, however, may not understand the need for accuracy and candor with health care providers (Myers, 1992). When a child does not understand that his or her well-being may be affected by statements made to a professional, the primary rationale for the diagnosis or treatment exception evaporates, and the judge may rule that the child's hearsay statements do not satisfy the exception.

The diagnosis or treatment exception applies to statements made to medical professionals, such as physicians and nurses. In a number of states, the exception also applies to statements to mental health professionals providing diagnostic and/or treatment services.

To increase the probability that a child's statements satisfy the requirements of the diagnosis or treatment exception, the professional can take the following steps.

1. Determine whether the child understands that the purpose of the interview or examination is to provide diagnosis and/or treatment. Document the child's understanding. In one case, an experienced pediatrician introduced herself to her 4-year-old patient and said, "I'm Dr. Bays, and I'm going to do a checkup to see how strong you are, how healthy you are, and if there's anything that needs to be done" (*State v. Logan*, 1991). The doctor's introduction informed the child of the purpose of the interview and examination, and helped persuade the court that the child's hearsay statements to the doctor met the requirements of the medical diagnosis or treatment exception.

If more than one professional interacts with a child during an assessment, they should determine whether the child understands that each professional is involved in the diagnostic or treatment process. Again, documentation is critical. In *State v. Logan*, mentioned in the preceding paragraph, the pediatrician conducted her physical examination and initial interview of the child and then introduced the child to a nonmedical colleague who conducted a videotaped interview. The pediatrician made sure the child knew that the nonphysician was part of the assessment team.

2. Emphasize to the child the importance of providing accurate information, and of being completely forthcoming. Document any information that indicates that the child understands the importance of accuracy.

3. The medical diagnosis or treatment exception requires that information supplied to the professional be pertinent to diagnosis or treatment. Thus the professional should document why information disclosed during the interview was pertinent to effective diagnosis or treatment.

4. If the child identifies the perpetrator during the interview, document why knowing the identity of the perpetrator was important for diagnostic and/or therapeutic reasons. For example, an emergency room physician needs to know who abused a child so the

doctor can ensure the child's safety. Protecting the child from continued abuse is an essential element of treatment. With some forms of abuse, the physician needs to test for sexually transmitted disease, and the identity of the abuser is pertinent. Mental health professionals beginning treatment for a child usually need to know who abused the child.

The medical diagnosis or treatment exception plays an important role in child abuse litigation, and documenting the information outlined above allows professionals to increase the likelihood that a child's hearsay statements will satisfy the requirements of the exception.

The residual and child hearsay exceptions. Many states have a hearsay exception known as a residual or catchall exception.[7] A residual exception allows use in court of reliable hearsay statements that do not meet the requirements of one of the more traditional hearsay exceptions, such as the excited utterance exception.

Beginning in 1982 in the state of Washington, legislatures have enacted special exceptions for hearsay statements of child abuse victims. These child hearsay exceptions are now on the books in a majority of states. The child hearsay exceptions are first cousins to residual exceptions, and, like residual exceptions, they allow use in court of reliable hearsay statements that do not satisfy the requirements of other hearsay exceptions.

When a child's hearsay statement is offered under a residual or child hearsay exception, the most important question is usually whether the statement is reliable. That is, is the statement true? The U.S. Supreme Court's decision in *Idaho v. Wright* (1990) has an important impact on the information judges consider when assessing the reliability of children's hearsay statements offered under residual and child hearsay exceptions. The Supreme Court ruled that judges should consider the totality of the circumstances in determining reliability. In considering the totality of the circumstances, however, the Supreme Court ruled that "the relevant circumstances include only those that surround the making of the statement" (p. 3148). Thus, when evaluating the reliability of a child's hearsay statement offered under a residual or child hearsay exception, the trial judge considers *only* those circumstances that immediately

Table 2.3 Factors Related to the Reliability of Children's Statements, and That Immediately Surround the Making of the Statements

- spontaneity
- questioning
- consistent statements
- child's state of mind and emotion
- play or gestures that support the child's description of abuse
- developmentally unusual knowledge of sexual acts or anatomy
- idiosyncratic details about sexual abuse
- use of developmentally appropriate terminology
- child's belief that disclosure might lead to punishment of the child
- child's or adult's motive to fabricate
- child's correction of the interviewer

surround the making of the statement. The judge does *not* consider evidence that does not immediately surround the statement, even though that evidence tends to corroborate the truth of the child's statement. For example, when a judge evaluates the reliability of a child's hearsay statement offered under a residual or child hearsay exception, the judge does *not* consider corroborating medical or physical evidence.

Professionals who interview and treat sexually abused children play an indispensable role in documenting the information judges consider as they assess the reliability of children's hearsay statements under residual and child hearsay exceptions. There is no litmus test for reliability, nor can reliability be reduced to a mathematical formula or test. Nevertheless, presence or absence of the following factors plays an important role in judicial assessment of reliability.

Spontaneity. Spontaneity is an important indicator of reliability. The more spontaneous a child's statement, the less likely it was a product of fabrication or distortion.

Statements elicited by questioning. The reliability of a child's hearsay statement may be influenced by the type of questions that elicited the statement. When questioning is leading, the possibility exists that the questioner influenced the child's statement, raising questions about reliability. As the Supreme Court pointed out in *Idaho v. Wright*, however, use of leading questions with children does not necessarily render their hearsay statements untrustworthy.

Consistent statements. Reliability may be enhanced when a child repeats a description of abuse more than once, and when the descriptions are consistent. If a child's recounting of events varies each time abuse is described, reliability may be questioned. This is not to say, however, that complete consistency is required for a child's hearsay statement to be reliable. What is important is consistency regarding the core details of the experience. Consistency about peripheral details is less important.

The dynamics of disclosure make consistency particularly tricky. Sorensen and Snow (1991) observe that disclosure of sexual abuse is a process, not an event. Many children disclose a little at a time. A person who does not understand child development and child abuse could mistakenly conclude that a child who tells slightly different stories at different times is not telling the truth. Knowledge of the disclosure process allows professionals to place inconsistency in perspective. (For further discussion of reasons for children's inconsistency, see Chapter 5.)

The child's state of mind and emotion when the hearsay statement is made. A child may display affect or emotion that supports the reliability of a hearsay statement. For example, an older child may demonstrate embarrassment or shame that one might expect upon disclosure of sexual abuse. Jones and McQuiston (1985) encourage interviewers to determine whether

> the child's account [is] given in a rehearsed or packaged manner or with appropriate emotion? Is the allegation delivered at the slightest cue from the interviewer, or in one or two sentences without the usual difficulty and reserve or hesitancy that children show? Is the emotion expressed genuinely experienced, or is it hollow in its manner of expression? Is the child bland, unemotive, and seemingly little perturbed by serious exploitation? (p. 30)

Some abused children are not emotional as they describe abuse. For example, a child who has described abuse five times to five different interviewers may have an understandably bland delivery. Furthermore, a child with dissociative symptoms may disclose without apparent emotion. Lack of affect may be a function of the child's psychological defense mechanism.

Play or gestures coinciding with a hearsay statement describing abuse. A young child's play or gestures while describing sexual abuse may enhance the reliability of the child's statement. For example, if a child places the penis of an anatomical doll in the mouth of another doll or in the child's mouth while describing sexual abuse, the child's verbal statement may gain trustworthiness.

Developmentally unusual knowledge of sexual acts or anatomy. Young children lack the experience required to fabricate detailed and anatomically accurate accounts of sexual acts (MacFarlane & Waterman, 1986). It is difficult to imagine a 4-year-old inventing a detailed and accurate account of fellatio, including ejaculation, unless the child has either experienced fellatio or seen it. Jones and McQuiston (1985) urge interviewers to "examine the statement for explicit detail of an alleged sexual abuse" (p. 29).

Naturally, care must be taken to rule out alternative explanations for a child's developmentally unusual knowledge of sexual acts or anatomy. Did parents talk to their child about sex? Did the child use words mentioned by interviewers? Did the child watch a pornographic videotape? Did the child observe adults or older siblings engaged in sexual behavior? The possibility that a child will observe sexual conduct at home may be higher for children living in crowded conditions (Everson & Boat, 1990).

Idiosyncratic detail. Presence in a child's statement of idiosyncratic details of sexual abuse points toward reliability. Jones and McQuiston (1985) write that "idiosyncrasy in the sexual abuse account is exemplified by children who describe smells and tastes associated with rectal, vaginal or oral sex" (p. 30). It is important to note, however, that lack of idiosyncratic detail does not make a description of abuse unreliable. Some forms of abuse lack unique detail. Fondling through clothing is an example. In some cases, paucity of detail is a function of a child's psychological defenses. In young children, difficulty with free-recall memory may limit the amount of detail in the child's description. (Children's memory is discussed more fully later in this chapter).

Use of developmentally appropriate terminology. When a young child's disclosure of abuse is made in words one would expect from a child of that age, the reliability of the statement may be enhanced. By contrast, if a child's disclosure employs adult terminology, the possibility of coaching arises. The child's choice of words is not a litmus test for reliability, however. Many abused children experience multiple interviews, and it is not uncommon for young children to pick up terms such as *molest* and *penetration* during the course of interviews, and to incorporate such terms into their descriptions of abuse. Similarly, an abused child who would not spontaneously use adult terminology may first reveal abuse to a parent, who introduces a term that seems unusual coming from the child. An abused child with a sophisticated vocabulary might use adultlike terms during initial disclosure. Thus in considering the child's terminology it is important to assess the child's developmental and linguistic level along with the number of times the child was interviewed and by whom.

Child's belief that disclosure might lead to punishment of the child. Children and adults often hesitate to make statements they believe will get them in trouble. If a child believed disclosing abuse could result in punishment or other unpleasant consequences, confidence in the child's statement may rise.

Child's or adult's motive to fabricate. Evidence that a child or an adult with access to the child had a motive to fabricate allegations of abuse can have an impact on reliability.

Correcting the interviewer. Reliability may be enhanced when a child does not agree with everything the interviewer asks, or when the child corrects the interviewer. Disagreement and correction demonstrate that the child has a firm mental picture of the abuse. Furthermore, disagreement indicates that the child is not simply responding unthinkingly, or answering questions to please the interviewer.

The foregoing factors are not the only indicators of reliability. Professionals should document *anything* supporting the conclusion that a child was telling the truth when describing sexual abuse.

In *Idaho v. Wright*, the Supreme Court ruled that when assessing the reliability of children's hearsay statements offered under residual or child hearsay exceptions, the judge may consider only those factors immediately surrounding the making of the hearsay statement. The judge may not consider evidence that does not immediately surround the making of the statement, even though that evidence bolsters confidence in the child's statement. The Supreme Court's ruling does not mean, however, that it is unimportant to document factors that do not immediately surround the making of the statement. For legal reasons beyond the scope of this book, it is *just as important* to document factors that do not immediately surround the child's statement as it is to document factors that do immediately surround the statement. Professionals should document the following factors that can corroborate the child's statement.

Medical evidence of abuse. A child's statement may be corroborated by medical evidence.

Changes in child's behavior. When a child's behavior alters in a way that corroborates the child's description of abuse, it may be appropriate to place increased confidence in the child's statement. For example, it would be important to note that a young child engaged in developmentally inappropriate sexual play with other children. Similarly, it is important to document symptoms of post-traumatic stress disorder. As my colleagues and I have noted:

> While some of the behaviors observed in sexually abused children are consistent with a number of problems, others are more strongly associated with personal or vicarious sexual experience. Examples of behaviors that have greater specificity for sexual abuse include . . . sexualization of play and behavior in young children, the appearance of genitalia in young children's drawings, and sexually explicit play with anatomically detailed dolls. (Myers et al., 1989, pp. 62-63; see also Faller, 1990; Sgroi, Porter, & Blick, 1982; Wyatt & Powell, 1988)

Table 2.4 Factors That Relate to Reliability but Usually Do Not Immediately Surround the Making of the Statement

---

- medical evidence of abuse
- changes in the child's behavior that indicate abuse
- more than one victim tells the same story
- corroboration by an eyewitness
- alleged perpetrator's opportunity to abuse the child
- admission by the alleged perpetrator
- evidence that the alleged perpetrator sexually abused other children

---

More than one victim tells the same story. Two or more children may be exposed to the same event. If the children are interviewed separately and both tell similar stories, their statements are mut- ually corroborative, enhancing the reliability of both. If, on the other hand, the children are interviewed together, the fact that they tell the same story does little to bolster the reliability of their individual statements, since one child may be influenced by the other.

Corroboration by an eyewitness. There are seldom eyewitnesses to sexual abuse. Nevertheless, in the rare case where someone happens to observe the incident, the eyewitness can corroborate the child's version of events, and bolster confidence in the child's hearsay statement.

Alleged perpetrator's opportunity to commit the abuse. The fact that the person accused of abuse had the opportunity to commit the abuse described by the child may increase the reliability of the child's statement.

Admission by alleged perpetrator. An admission or confession by the alleged perpetrator corroborates the child's statement.

Evidence that the alleged perpetrator sexually abused other children. Evidence that the alleged perpetrator has a history of sexually abusing children may support a child's hearsay statement describing sexual abuse.

The Importance of Documentation

Interviewers are in a peerless position to record children's hearsay statements *and* to document the factors judges consider to determine whether hearsay statements meet the requirements of a hearsay exception. By taking a few moments to document the factors discussed above, professionals substantially increase the probability that a child's hearsay statements can be used in later legal proceedings.

It is impossible to emphasize too strongly the importance of documentation. The legal proceeding at which a child's hearsay statements are needed may occur months or even years after the child discloses abuse. Unless there is careful documentation of *exactly* what questions were asked and *exactly* what the child said, there is very little chance the professional will remember when he or she is called as a witness and asked to repeat the child's hearsay statement. A vague recollection of what a child said will *not* do. Paraphrasing what children say may be acceptable sometimes, but more often than not, the law requires the exact words spoken by the child. Only detailed documentation holds any realistic promise of preserving the detail the law requires.

> *It is impossible to emphasize too strongly the importance of documentation.*

Documentation is needed not only to preserve the child's words, but also to preserve a record of the factors that indicate whether a child's hearsay statement meets the requirements of an exception to the hearsay rule.

DOCUMENTING INFORMATION ON
THE CHILD'S COMPETENCE TO BE A WITNESS

In former days, judges often ruled that children could not testify as witnesses (Myers, 1992). Children were said to be testimonially incompetent. Today, children are generally allowed to testify, and children as young as 3 years old take the witness stand. When questions arise about the capacity of a particular child to testify, the

judge determines whether the child possesses the following characteristics:

1. capacity to observe events
2. sufficient memory to recall events
3. ability to communicate
4. ability to distinguish fact from fantasy
5. understanding of the difference between the truth and a lie, and appreciation that it is wrong to lie

Interviewers should watch for and document information relating to these capacities. Such information can be obtained without a
lot of additional questions. As the interview proceeds, the professional can simply note the child's ability to observe, remember, and
describe events. It is easy to document that the child is similar to
other children in these capacities.

During the interview, the child may say that something is "just
pretend" or "just on TV." Such statements indicate awareness of the
distinction between real and pretend, and can be noted. (Discussion
of children's ability to distinguish fact from fantasy is presented
later in this chapter.)

Finally, a few simple questions can demonstrate the child's understanding of the difference between the truth and a lie, and the
consequences of telling a lie.

It is important for the interviewer to document the characteristics
a judge uses to decide on a child's capacity to testify, for three reasons.
First, quite apart from whether the child ever testifies, the characteristics are relevant in deciding whether the child's disclosure is
trustworthy. Second, information on the child's capacities can be
shared with the attorney who is trying to determine whether the child
is capable of testifying. Finally, some types of hearsay statements
are admissible in court only if the person who made the statement
had the capacity to testify as a witness *at the time* the hearsay statement was made. Thus if the child makes a hearsay statement during
the interview, the ability to use the statement in court may depend
on whether the child possessed the capacities discussed above *at the
time* of the interview.

CONCLUSION

It is clear that there are far-reaching legal implications of what children say during interviews. Professionals should realize, however, that the hearsay issues discussed in this chapter are just the tip of the legal iceberg. Children's statements made during interviews can be used in court for other important purposes as well. By taking the simple step of recording what goes on during interviews, professionals preserve invaluable evidence that can protect children.

❑ **Steps Toward
Forensically Defensible Interviews**

This section presents a discussion of interview techniques that are forensically defensible. The section is *not* intended to represent a rigid set of rules that must be followed by professionals who interview children. Every professional develops a unique style of interviewing, and that is all to the good. There never was and never will be one "correct" way to talk to children. Although there is no panacea when it comes to interviewing, there are some things to avoid. The following pages offer general guidance on the important legal implications of interviews with children.

THE CONTINUUM OF
QUESTIONING TECHNIQUES, WITH
PARTICULAR EMPHASIS ON LEADING QUESTIONS

No aspect of the escalating attack on interviewers causes more anxiety than criticism of leading questions. With this concern in mind, this section dwells at some length on the various types of questions used during interviews, particularly leading questions.

For professionals who interview or treat sexually abused children, leading questions are like a 5-year-old's monster under the bed: an ill-defined and brooding ogre that waits to pounce when the light goes out. The mere mention of leading questions makes professionals squirm. Why do we squirm? In part because no one knows quite

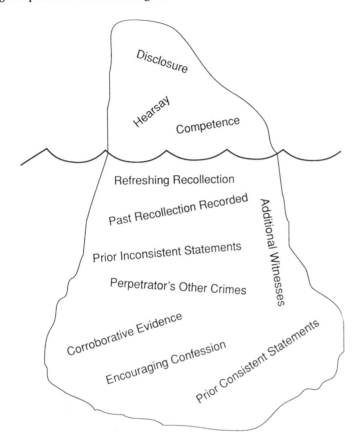

Figure 2.1. The Legal Iceberg

what a leading question looks like! If only we knew what leading questions looked like, we could avoid them. But leading questions are as difficult to define as they are to avoid. One reason, therefore, for professional anxiety is that it is often difficult to tell when a question is leading and when it is not. A second source of concern is the reality that the use of leading questions can have serious legal consequences.

The starting place for analysis of leading questions is a definition: A leading question is a question that contains a suggestion of what the answer should be. A leading question, then, is a suggestive question, a question that tempts the child to give a particular answer —for example, It sure is cold out today, isn't it? The question prompts the child to agree with the questioner. Leading questions take many forms, from strongly leading, like the question about the weather, to mildly leading. To complicate matters, a question that is leading in one context may be nonleading in another.

It is useful to contrast leading questions with other types of questions (for information on questioning techniques, see Faller, 1990, chap. 5). An *open-ended* question invites a child to discuss whatever the child wants to discuss about a subject. Examples of open-ended questions include the following: Has anything been happening? Do you know why we are talking today? Can you tell me about that? Did anything happen? An open-ended question is little more than an invitation to speak.

A *focused* question is more specific than an open-ended question. A focused question draws a child's attention to a particular person, place, time, or event, or introduces a new topic for discussion. An example of a focused question is, Shall we talk about preschool now? The question directs the child's attention to a new subject, but does not suggest that the questioner wants any particular information about preschool.

Focused questions are legitimate and, in most cases, indispensable during interviews of children and adults alike. But when does a focused question cross the line and become a leading question? That is, when does a question suggest a particular answer? There is no clear line separating focused from leading questions. Almost any question can lead to some degree. Questions are always on a continuum of suggestiveness. At one end of the continuum is the open-ended question. At the other end is the *coercive* question, which intimidates or threatens a child into providing a specific answer.

White and Quinn (1988) offer useful illustrations of questions that may coerce children. Asking a question repeatedly until the child gives the "right" answer can be coercive. When repetition is necessary, Davies and Montegna (1990) suggest, "change your vocabulary or the way you phrase the question" (p. 8). Rejecting a child's answer or insisting that the child provide another answer can coerce.

White and Quinn (1988) warn against offering children tangible rewards: "Such techniques may be seen as attempts to bribe or

Less Suggestive Questions

open-ended

focused

leading

coercive

More Suggestive Questions

Figure 2.2. The Continuum of Suggestibility

coerce the child into giving information, even if the treat has not been given with such an intention" (p. 275). This does not mean professionals can never offer a child a cup of juice. It is sometimes useful, for example, to offer a child refreshment prior to the interview. Moreover, a child may be given something to eat or drink when the interview is over. Indeed, research indicates that a child may be better able to resist suggestive questions when he or she is comfortable and the interviewer is friendly (Goodman, Rudy, Bottoms, & Aman, 1990, p. 278).

Although it is appropriate to praise a child for "working hard" or "doing a good job" during the interview, praise should center on the child's effort rather than the content of what the child says. As Saywitz, Geiselman, and Bornstein (in press) write: "It is a good idea to praise children for their effort. . . . It is *not* a good idea to praise them for the content of what they report, as this may cause them to 'report more of the same' whether they are certain about the information or not" (app. B).

The interviewer should not tell the child that he or she can "earn" something to eat or drink by cooperating. Children should not be told they cannot go to the bathroom or see a parent until they tell the interviewer what happened. Such techniques are coercive and improper.

Definitions of open-ended, focused, leading, and coercive questions are useful, but only to a point. When a professional talks to a child, the dynamics of the interview change so quickly that there is seldom time to match questions against definitions. Fortunately, interviewers do not have to pause before each question and compare the question against some definitional yardstick. The most accurate barometer of "leadingness" is a commonsense assessment of how strongly a question tempts a child to give a particular answer.

A few examples help to illustrate leading questions:

Your daddy touched your pee-pee. Isn't that right?

The unspoken message is clear: Say yes. In a sense, this is not a question at all. It is a statement of fact followed by a request for agreement. Such "requests" can have a powerful influence on children and adults alike. The "question" is little more than an afterthought tagged on at the end. Such *tag* questions are highly leading.

Consider this question:

Your daddy touched your pee-pee, didn't he?

This is a tag question too. Such questions should be avoided because they are highly leading.

How about this question:

Did your daddy touch your pee-pee?

Clearly, this question is not as strongly suggestive as the tag questions, but does the question lead? Does it suggest a particular answer? The context in which the question is asked may make this question mildly to moderately leading. To determine whether or not a question is leading, one has to know whether the question was asked in a suggestive manner. One also has to examine the questions that led up to the question to see whether the context of the conversation gave the child a hint that the interviewer wanted a particular answer.

Here is another example: Suppose that abuse is suspected, but the child has not disclosed. The interviewer's *first* question focused on abuse is:

Can you tell me what happened?

When this is the *first* question focused on abuse, an argument can be made that it is suggestive. The question does not ask *whether* something happened. Instead, the question *assumes* something happened. When the child hears this question, he or she thinks, "The grown-up thinks 'something' happened, so maybe 'something' did." The question is not neutral, and the child may be tempted to go along with the adult *whether "something" happened or not*. If this question is postponed until the child begins disclosing, it is much harder to argue that it is suggestive.

As mentioned earlier, there is no litmus test to differentiate leading from nonleading questions. Two practical guidelines are useful, however. First, questions beginning with *is, are, were, do,* and *did* are often mildly leading. Second, questions that call for yes or no answers are often leading.

When the professional's experience and knowledge of child development tell him or her, *deep down inside,* that a question tempts a child to answer in a particular way, the question is probably leading to some degree. That does not necessarily mean the question should not be asked. It does mean, however, that the interviewer's level of concern should rise a notch or two.

The consensus of professional opinion is that the interviewer should begin by "establishing an atmosphere in which the child feels comfortable and free to talk" (Saywitz, Goodman, & Myers, 1990, p. 1). Initial questioning should be as nonfocused and nonleading as possible. Information provided in response to open-ended questions may be more accurate—although less complete—than information provided in response to specific questions (Saywitz, Geiselman, & Bornstein, in press).

The interviewer should begin with nonfocused, open-ended questions that invite spontaneous statements. Resist the temptation to interrupt the child. Allow the child time to formulate an answer before moving on to the next question. As Saywitz, Geiselman, & Bornstein, (in press) advise, "Do not ask the child a string of questions without waiting for a response" (app. C). If the child does not respond to generic, open-ended questions—and many children do not—then the interviewer will need to focus the child's attention on a particular topic. When focused questions are used, the interviewer proceeds along a continuum, usually beginning with questions that simply focus the child's attention on a particular subject, and, when necessary, moving gradually to more specific questions. Highly specific questions sometimes cross the line into leading questions.

Some professionals may be skeptical of advice to begin interviews of young children with open-ended questions such as Why are we here today? Few young children disclose in response to such questions, and some interviewers may feel that open-ended questions are a waste of time. But just as physicians practice defensive medicine to avoid legal problems, so can professionals immunize themselves from legal challenge by beginning with open-ended questions. A defense attorney has difficulty attacking an interviewer who begins with open-ended questions and then moves to focused and, finally, mildly leading questions only when open-ended questions do not work. Even though the interviewer knows ahead of time that open-ended questions may not work, there is little to lose and much to gain—forensically speaking—by starting with open-ended questions.

When there is no alternative but to resort to mildly leading questions, they should be questions that do not mention the suspected abuser or the location where abuse occurred. For example, if the interviewer suspects that abuse occurred in the bathroom and that the child's father is the perpetrator, he or she might ask, "Did it happen at McDonald's?" The child will reject this "silly" question, and may spontaneously reveal, "It happened in the bathroom." To help the child disclose the identity of the perpetrator, the interviewer might say, "Is the person who hurt you on TV sometimes?" This question is relatively benign, and it provides the child an opportunity to be the first to mention the perpetrator's name.

Boat and Everson (1988) provide a useful approach when open-ended questions do not work. They conceptualize the interview as a continuum involving "levels of escalation." The first level involves questions about "critical events or times in the child's life when the

Less Suggestive Questions

mildly focused

strongly focused

mildly leading

strongly leading

More Suggestive Questions

Figure 2.3. Suggestibility of Focused and Leading Questions

abuse most likely occurred" (p. 348). If the child discloses sexual abuse at this level, further escalation is unnecessary. If disclosure is halting or not forthcoming, the interviewer proceeds to the second level of escalation, in which "the child is asked in general terms about the particular individual or individuals who are suspected of being the perpetrators of the abuse" (p. 348). At this level, Boat and Everson advise interviewers to avoid direct reference to abuse or sexual matters. If further escalation is required, the third level entails direct questions about abuse:

> This level of inquiry represents an escalation in the interview in that the child is now asked directly about possible abuse rather than being encouraged to disclose it spontaneously. This level is used when it is clear that the more subtle and indirect approaches are not productive. The child should be asked directly about several types of sexual abuse, but only in general terms. The name of the alleged perpetrator is never introduced by the interviewer. (pp. 348-349)

If the child denies abuse at the third level of escalation, Boat and Everson advise bringing the interview to a close. They acknowledge, however, that there are times when further escalation is necessary, and describe a fourth level of escalation in which it is sometimes "necessary to risk asking the child potentially leading or suggestive questions in order to obtain enough evidence to intervene to protect the child. This is especially true when there is strong evidence of sexual abuse from other sources, but the child seems too anxious or frightened to talk openly about it" (p. 349).

Although leading questions should be avoided when possible, cogent situational and developmental reasons support occasional use of highly focused and even mildly leading questions. The situational dynamics of sexual abuse often work against disclosure. Many children are threatened into silence. Others are ambivalent about disclosure. In Sorensen and Snow's (1991) study of disclosure in 116 cases of confirmed sexual abuse, 79% of the children "initially denied their abuse or were tentative in disclosing it" (p. 12). Sorensen and Snow conclude that "disclosure of child sexual abuse is best described . . . as a process, not an event. The common presumption that most abused children are capable of immediate active disclosure" is unwarranted (p. 11).

Strategies exist to help avoidant children disclose. For example, Davies and Montegna (1990) advise interviewers "to reassure children that they are not in trouble, that they have done nothing wrong, and that nothing they feel or say will make you embarrassed, upset, or critical of them" (p. 8). Allow children time to disclose. For example, some children are more comfortable beginning with peripheral details, and moving gradually to central events. Children's anxiety can be lowered by allowing periods of free play between questions about abuse.

The situational dynamics of sexual abuse are not the only barriers to disclosure. As explained more fully below, the developmental immaturity of young children further complicates the interview process. Young children are not as adept as older children at remembering events in response to generic, open-ended questions such as Did something happen? Ask a 4-year-old, "What happened at preschool today?" and the answer is, predictably, "Nothing" or "I played." It is not that the youngster does not remember. Rather, young children often need cues to trigger specific memories. A focused or leading question may provide the trigger needed to help a child remember details of an experience.

When mildly leading questions are postponed until other methods of questioning have proven unsuccessful, the interviewer is warranted in asking such questions. Naturally, if disclosure is forthcoming without leading questions, it is usually wise to forgo such questions. In the final analysis, however, when mildly leading questions are employed with circumspection, they can be defended on legal as well as psychological grounds. This is not to say, of course, that responsible and circumspect use of mildly leading questions is immune from attack. A professional who finds it necessary to ask a few mildly leading questions should not be surprised when a defense attorney challenges him or her and argues that the professional's technique renders the child's disclosure unreliable. The point is that professionals can defend against such attacks by explaining the situational and developmental reasons supporting cautious use of focused and even mildly leading questions.

Defending occasional use of mildly leading questions requires an understanding of children's memory, suggestibility, and ability to distinguish fact from fantasy. The following discussion draws heavily on the work of Gail S. Goodman, Ph.D., of the State University of New York at Buffalo and Karen J. Saywitz, Ph.D., of the Harbor/UCLA Medical Center in Los Angeles.

It is important to keep in mind that across ages, children vary widely in their abilities. A 2-year-old has different abilities from a 5-year-old, and a 5-year-old has different abilities from a 10-year-old. It is equally important to remember that children of the same age can differ markedly. One 3-year-old is an excellent reporter of events, while another says nothing. Thus, in considering children's ability to describe events, professionals should not treat children as a uniform group.

Taken as a whole, research and theory on child development suggest that children, like adults, bring strengths and weaknesses to the interview room. Children demonstrate adultlike reliability when providing certain kinds of information, under certain conditions. In other situations, children perform less well than adults. To complicate matters further, there are some conditions in which children actually outperform adults. For example, children sometimes observe details that adults overlook. Thus it is a mistake to conclude that children are uniformly less reliable reporters of events than adults.

Memory

Young children possess the memory skills needed to describe events, especially when they are asked simple questions in a supportive atmosphere (Fivush, in press; Fivush, Gray, & Fromhoff, 1987; Fivush & Hamond, 1990; Flin, Boon, Knox, & Bull, 1992; Hamond & Fivush, 1991; Hudson & Fivush, 1990, 1991; Melton, Petrila, Poythress, & Slobogin, 1987). Children remember familiar as well as novel events (Nelson, 1986). Participation in an event generally leads to better recall than mere observation (Goodman et al., 1990; Tobey & Goodman, in press). Traumatic and stressful events are remembered (Goodman, Hirschman, Hepps, & Rudy, 1991; Jones & Krugman, 1986; Pynoos & Eth, 1984; Spencer & Flin, 1990; Terr, 1988). In several studies, researchers have found that memory for stressful events is stronger than memory for nonstressful events (Goodman et al., 1990); other research suggests that stress may impair memory (Peters, 1987, 1991; Saywitz & Nathanson, 1992). In general, memory for the gist of events is more enduring than memory for details.

When considering children's memory, it is useful to consider two types of memory: free recall and recognition (Perry & Wrightsman, 1991; Sivan, 1991). Recognition memory is at work when cues trigger the child's memory for an event. Perry (1987) notes that "recognition is the simplest form of remembering because it requires only that we perceive an object as something that was perceived previously." Thus when a child picks a suspect from a police lineup, the suspect triggers the child's recollection. Recognition memory develops very early in life (Perry, 1987).

A child relies on free recall when remembering an event *without* the assistance of memory cues. Perry (1987) writes that "recall is the most complex form of memory. It requires that previously observed events be retrieved from memory with few or no prompts. It also is the form of retrieval often required of witnesses" (p. 491). Thus a child uses free recall when he or she is asked, What happened a week ago? Free-recall memory involves complex cognitive processes that develop gradually.

One of the most stable findings of research on children's memory is that when young children are asked open-ended questions requiring free recall—such as What happened?—they spontaneously recall less information than do older children and adults (Goodman et al., 1990; Saywitz, Goodman, & Myers, 1990; Spencer & Flin, 1990). This is not to say that young children remember less, but that young children are not as proficient at free recall as are older children and adults. Spencer and Flin (1990) summarize the psychological research:

> To date, research has shown clearly that the most salient and consistent age difference in witnessing is found when the memory test is free recall. This means that the subject is asked to recount everything he or she remembers without prompting, such as "Describe everything you saw." In response to this type of questioning, younger children typically report less information than older children and adults, but most significantly, the information they do recall is generally accurate.
>
> Thus there appear to be age differences in the *quantity* of freely recalled details but not in the *quality* (accuracy). . . .
>
> In a typical forensic context, free recall and very general questions are of limited use and interviewers need to use more specific questions in order to elicit the maximum amount of information. (p. 240)

As Spencer and Flin observe, the difficulty young children experience with free recall means such children often require memory cues to help them remember (Dent, 1990). Whereas an adult or older child might be able to provide a detailed account in response to an open-ended question like Did anything happen? young children often need specific questions to trigger "recognition memory."

Passage of time takes its toll on memory. Spencer and Flin (1990) write:

> Both adults' and children's memories are highly sensitive to the passage of time. Although some knowledge and experiences are stored for decades, a great deal of information is lost or becomes inaccessible due to decay or interference.
>
> . . .
>
> Lawyers generally assume that children's memories fade faster than adults'. It is now widely accepted that children, including very young children, can be as reliable in their recollections of events as adults. However, it also seems to be generally accepted that a child's capacity for recall, especially on points of detail, may deteriorate more rapidly

over time than would that of an adult. This seems to be particularly the case with young children. (p. 250)

Children who are asked to talk about events they have experienced tend to omit information they know about more often than they mistakenly report events that did not occur. That is, children are more likely to forget details than to invent or fantasize details that did not happen.

The work of Saywitz, Geiselman, and Borenstein (in press) on the effects of cognitive interviewing on 7- to 11-year-old children's memory holds promise for improving children's ability to recall details of events. These researchers offer techniques that can be used to help children jog their memories. First, at an appropriate time during the interview, children may be encouraged to reconstruct the event mentally. The interviewer may say, "Picture that time when you were at grandpa's house. Think about what it was like. What did the room look like? What things were in the room?" Saywitz and her colleagues suggest that the interviewer ask the child to describe the mental construction out loud, to be sure the child expends the necessary mental effort. Dent (1990) emphasizes that mentally reconstructing the event is "the most obvious productive interviewing strategy. Ask the children to recount the appropriate day's activities from some point to the point in which the incident occurred" (p. 289).

When an important subject is broached during the interview, Saywitz, Geiselman, and Bornstein (in press) suggest that the interviewer tell the child:

> Now I want you to start at the beginning and tell me what happened, from the beginning to the middle, to the end. Tell me everything you remember, even little parts that you don't think are very important. Sometimes people leave out little things because they think little things are not important. Tell me everything that happened. (app. B)

Sometimes children's memories can be triggered by asking them to remember events backward. The interviewer might ask the child to think of the last thing that happened, then the middle, then the beginning, reminding the child to avoid skipping steps. Saywitz and her colleagues recommend saying to children, "Then what happened *right* before that?" (app. B).

The research of Saywitz and her colleagues discloses that the memory-enhancing techniques described above are successful in helping children remember details they would otherwise not recall. Of equal importance, the techniques do not appear to increase 7- to 11-year-old children's suggestibility.

In the final analysis, young children can remember what they experience. They may need help to do so, however, which raises the specter of suggestibility.

Suggestibility

Are young children so suggestible that their descriptions of sexual abuse cannot be trusted? Many adults believe children are highly suggestible. Psychological research conducted in Europe during the first quarter of this century fueled this belief (Goodman, 1984). One early writer stated, "Create, if you will, an idea of what the child is to hear or see, and the child is very likely to hear or see what you desire" (Brown, 1926). Freud added to doubts about children's credibility with his belief that women and girls commonly fantasize sexual assault (Myers, 1992; Summit, 1988). In recent years, Freud's theories have been criticized, and psychologists have conducted more rigorous study of children's suggestibility. Contemporary psychological research is exploding the old bromide that children are dangerously suggestible (Goodman & Clarke-Stewart, 1991).

Some studies of suggestibility present children with artificial stimuli such as stories or pictures of innocuous events, and then test the effect of leading questions on how well the children remember the stimuli. Increasingly, however, psychologists design experiments that present children with more realistic and personally meaningful events (Goodman & Clarke-Stewart, 1991; Goodman et al., 1990). Experiments that employ greater "ecological validity" provide greater insight into children's memory and suggestibility regarding real-life events (Ceci, 1991). Spencer and Flin (1990) write:

> The most useful research studies are those which have examined the influence of suggestive questioning when children are asked to give

an account of a real event which they have witnessed. While attempts to measure children's susceptibility to suggestion when being questioned on their memory for a story or pictures may have theoretical value, these laboratory experiments represent too few of the relevant characteristics to be of real forensic significance. (p. 253)

Overall, psychological studies do not converge on a simple relation between age and suggestibility (Zaragoza, 1987). It is clear, however, that children are not always more suggestible than adults (Goodman et al., 1990). Suggestibility depends on cognitive, social, emotional, and situational factors, including level of interest or salience of the event (Goodman et al., 1990; Goodman & Schwartz-Kenney, in press; Matthews & Saywitz, 1992).

Research has shown that 10- and 11-year-olds appear to be no more suggestible than older children and adults (Goodman et al., 1990). Even 3-year-olds are not always more suggestible than older children, although there does appear to be a greater risk of suggestibility in very young children (Ceci, Ross, & Toglia, 1987; Goodman & Aman, 1990; Goodman & Reed, 1986).

Children are more suggestible regarding peripheral details of events than about key aspects (Goodman & Reed, 1986). Peripheral details are not remembered as well as key aspects, thus memory for peripheral details fades quickly, and, as memory fades, suggestibility increases. Participation in an event, as opposed to mere observation, sometimes lowers suggestibility about the event (Goodman et al., 1990).

The danger of obtaining inaccurate information in response to suggestive questions appears to be particularly high when children are asked to interpret ambiguous events (Goodman & Clarke-Stewart, 1991). When children do not know the meaning of an ambiguous event, they may acquiesce in an adult's interpretation. It should be noted, however, that although children may go along with suggestive questions about the *meaning* of ambiguous events, children are less susceptible to suggestion regarding the *facts* they observe. That is, children are more easily led astray regarding the meaning of ambiguous events than about *what* happened.

The finding that children have difficulty resisting leading questions about the meaning of ambiguous events has obvious implications for the interviewing of children. Greater confidence can be placed in children's descriptions of events than in children's interpretations of what happened. As Spencer and Flin (1990) note:

> Children are more influenced by leading questions: (a) when being asked about descriptions of people or things, rather than events; (b) when they are pressed to provide additional details; (c) when they do not have a good memory of the information in question; (d) after a long delay; (e) when the interview is stressful; and (f) when the interviewer lacks appropriate skills. (p. 254)

Suggestibility can be lowered by informing children that it is important to pay close attention to questions, and letting children know they should report only what they "really remember" (Warren, Hulse-Trotter, & Tubbs, 1991). Children benefit from being told that certain questions may be difficult or tricky, and that they should not answer unless they understand (Saywitz, Moan, & Lamphear, 1991). Dent (1990) advises telling children that the interviewer does not know what happened, and that children are free to say "I don't know." The interviewer may remind a child that the interviewer was not there when events occurred, and therefore does not know what happened (Saywitz, Moan, & Lamphear, 1991). In Saywitz, Moan, and Lamphear's (1991) research on helping children resist suggestive questions, they taught children "to use self statements, such as 'I knew there might be questions like this, I can do it.' [Children] were taught to roll back the tape of the event in their minds to compare their memory to the adults' suggestion before answering. They practiced saying 'stop and think' to themselves, so they didn't hurry into a wrong answer" (p. 7).

Saywitz, Geiselman, and Bornstein (in press) provide the following instructions, which may be given to children prior to the interview:

1. There may be some questions that you do not know the answers to. That's okay. Nobody can remember everything. If you don't know the answer to a question, then tell me "I don't know," but do not guess or make anything up. It is very important to tell me only what you really remember. Only what really happened.

2. If you do not want to answer some of the questions, you don't have to. That's okay. Tell me "I don't want to answer that question."

3. If you don't know what something I ask you means, tell me "I don't understand" or "I don't know what you mean." Tell me to say it in new words.

4. I may ask you some questions more than one time. Sometimes I forget that I already asked you that question. You don't have to change your answer, just tell me what you remember the best you can. (app. A)

Although there is a risk of obtaining inaccurate information with suggestive questions, there is a risk in *not* asking such questions. For example, when sensitive or embarrassing topics are involved, mildly leading questions may be necessary. A study by Saywitz, Goodman, Nicholas, and Moan (1991) illustrates the need to use mildly suggestive questions to elicit embarrassing information. The researchers studied nonabused 5- and 7-year-old girls who experienced a routine medical examination by a pediatrician. As part of the examination, half the girls received an external inspection of the vaginal and anal areas. The other half did not have the vaginal and anal examination. Some time later, all the children were questioned about the entire examination. Questioning began with questions like "What happened?" Then the children were asked focused and mildly suggestive questions, including questions about whether their vaginal and anal areas were examined.

Most of the children who experienced the vaginal and anal examination did not disclose the examination in response to open-ended questions like "What happened?" The majority of children disclosed the vaginal or anal examination only when they were asked mildly suggestive questions such as "Did the doctor touch you there?"

Of the children in the study who did not receive a vaginal and anal examination, the great majority (92%) resisted suggestive questions about such an examination. Only three children (8%) said they received a vaginal and anal examination when they did not. This research indicates that although there is a small risk of obtaining inaccurate information when mildly leading questions are asked, there is a greater risk that potentially embarrassing but truthful information will not be revealed unless mildly leading questions are asked.

Many sexually abused children are threatened into silence. The twin forces of embarrassment and fear of disclosure combine to justify occasional use of mildly suggestive questions during interviews. As Spencer and Flin (1990) observe, "Child witnesses in particular, do not voluntarily recite full and spontaneous accounts of their experiences or observations without some degree of prompting" (p. 276). Judges routinely allow leading questions when children testify in court (Myers, 1992), and similar flexibility must be tolerated during interviews of children who may be sexually abused.

The concern is often expressed that suggestibility is increased by the child's deference to the authority of the interviewer. There is evidence that children are more suggestible when interviewed by an authority figure (Ceci et al., 1987), but there is also evidence to the contrary (Brigham, Van Verst, & Bothwell, 1986). Goodman, Bottoms, Schwartz-Kenney, and Rudy (1991) found that the negative effect of authority on suggestibility can be lowered by establishing a warm and friendly rapport with children. That is, children are *less* suggestible when they feel safe and comfortable.

In summary, the evidence to date indicates that concern about suggestibility in children is warranted (Garbarino & Stott, 1989). At the same time, however, children are more resistant to suggestive questions than is commonly believed. Moreover, children do not have a corner on the suggestibility market—adults are suggestible too. Goodman and Clarke-Stewart (1991) summarize much of the research on the effect of leading questions on children:

There are dangers as well as benefits in the use of leading questions with children. The benefits appear in the finding . . . that leading questions were often necessary to elicit information from children about actual events they had experienced. . . .

The dangers of suggestive questioning lie in children's adding erroneous information to their accounts of what has occurred. The children in the studies by Goodman and her associates were generally accurate in reporting specific and personal things that had happened to them. If these results can be generalized to investigations of abuse, they suggest that normal children are unlikely to make up details of sexual acts when nothing abusive happened. They suggest that children will not easily yield to an interviewer's suggestion that something sexual occurred when in fact it did not, especially if nonintimidating interviewers ask questions children can comprehend. However, leading questions in these studies also resulted in a small number of children making errors that could be misinterpreted as suggesting that abuse had occurred.

A small number of children also made errors in reporting the details of what they had seen in the studies. . . . These errors were in line with suggestive questioning by a biased interviewer. In addition, . . . even those children who reported the facts accurately were swayed in their overall interpretation of events. If these findings can be generalized to abuse investigations, they suggest that young children might be led to mislabel or misinterpret acts when something nonabusive occurred that could be confused with abuse. Children do not make up facts often, . . . but . . . children can be led by a persistent interrogator to change their descriptions of what they have seen or what has been done if the event is somewhat ambiguous to start.

We can conclude that children are especially likely to accept an interviewer's suggestions when they are younger, when they are interrogated after a long delay, when they feel intimidated by the interviewer, when the interviewer's suggestions are strongly stated and frequently repeated, and when more than one interviewer makes the same strong suggestions. (p. 103)

Differentiating the Truth From a Lie and Fact From Fantasy

Children understand the difference between truth and falsehood. Although the young child's comprehension of the difference between the truth and a lie is concrete compared with older children and adults, young children understand the difference (Bussey, 1992; Haugaard, Reppucci, Laird, & Nauful, 1991; Kit-fong Au, 1992; MacFarlane & Waterman, 1986; Strichartz & Burton, 1990). This is not to say, however, that young children can respond to questions such as, "What is the difference between the truth and a lie?" Most children under age 5 do not understand the word *difference* (Matthews & Saywitz, 1992).

Children as young as 1½ are capable of misstating the truth. Although preschool and elementary school-aged children lie, "there is no evidence that honesty increases with age. . . . This means that children, like adults, may lie, but that there is no need to be more concerned about lying among children" (Berliner, 1988, p. 48). Melton (1981) notes that "there is in fact little correlation between age and honesty" (p. 79). Spencer and Flin (1990) add that "children and adults do tell lies, but there is no evidence to support the contention that children are more likely to lie than adults" (p. 270).

Although young children lie, they are not very good at it. Young children have difficulty maintaining conscious fabrication over time (Yates & Musty, 1988). Quinn (1988) observes that "current studies indicate that children under seven are unlikely to be successful telling a lie. By fourth and fifth grade, however, children become more proficient at telling lies" (p. 181).

Situational factors influence the moral decisions of adults and children (Hall, Lamb, & Perlmutter, 1986; Spencer & Flin, 1990). A child's decision to stray from the truth or engage in other improper behavior may be influenced by peer pressure, pressure from influential adults, the likelihood of detection, motive to fabricate, desire to engage in the prohibited activity, and attempts to escape blame or punishment. Every parent knows that normal, happy 3- and 4-year-olds often deny guilt when caught red-handed in the cookie jar.

The capacity to understand the difference between truth and falsehood is related to the ability to differentiate fact from fantasy. A child who cannot distinguish what actually happened from what he or she imagined cannot, in that instance, differentiate truth from falsity. Although imagination plays an important part in children's lives, children can separate what they experience from what they imagine (Saywitz, Goodman, & Myers, 1990; Sivan, 1991). Spencer and Flin (1990) write:

> There is no doubt that play and make-believe are an important part of a child's development. . . . But it should be remembered that adults also fantasize and daydream. And the critical issue is not whether children engage in imaginative games, but whether they are unable to distinguish fact from fantasy in the context of a witnessed offense. . . .
> The only relevant laboratory studies suggest that children do not show a general tendency to confuse what they have imagined or done with what they have perceived [Johnson & Foley, 1984; Lindsay & Johnson, 1987]. The only age difference found was that children were inferior to adults at discriminating real actions they themselves had performed from their imagined actions. However, the actions which the children performed (e.g., saying a word out loud or touching their elbow) bore little resemblance to the typical events of a crime. The artificiality of the stimuli and the fact that children were instructed to

imagine rather than using spontaneous imagination, seriously limit the forensic applications of their conclusions, a criticism acknowledged by the researchers.

There is certainly no psychological research or medical case study material which suggests that children are in the habit of fantasizing about the sort of incidents that might result in court proceedings: for example, observing road accidents or being indecently assaulted. Children's fantasies and play are characterized by their daily experience and personal knowledge, and unusual fantasies are seen by psychiatrists as highly suspicious: "The cognitive and imaginative capacities of three-year-olds do not enable them to describe anal intercourse and spitting out ejaculate, for instance. Such detailed descriptions from small children, in the absence of other factors, should be seen as stemming from the reality of past abuse rather than from their imagination." (pp. 258-259)

Summary

The child development literature indicates that young children possess the capacity to remember and relate events. Moreover, although young children are more suggestible than adults in some circumstances, children are not as suggestible as many adults believe, and in some studies, young children have been shown to be quite resistant to suggestive and misleading questioning. Finally, children can usually differentiate the real from the pretend.

Children, like adults, can be misled by leading and suggestive questions, and professionals who interview young children should use such questions sparingly. In some cases, however, highly focused and even mildly leading questions are required to enable traumatized and frightened children to describe events. As the number of focused and mildly leading questions rises, so does concern about the reliability of what children say. This is not to suggest, however, that such questions necessarily render children's statements unreliable. Many answers to leading questions are accurate.

INTERVIEWER OBJECTIVITY

Some critics of interview practices argue that interviewers should know nothing about the child before the interview begins. The critics assert that if the interviewer knows about the case in advance, he or she will bias the results. This argument is without merit.

The long-standing practice among professionals who interview sexually abused children is to obtain background information before the interview begins (American Professional Society on the Abuse of Children, 1990). Possession of background information does not necessarily bias the interviewer or make it impossible for him or her to elicit trustworthy information. It is true that interviewers must reject such preconceptions as "Children don't lie about sexual abuse." It is equally true that an interviewer should not begin an interview with his or her mind already made up. There is an important distinction, however, between preconceptions that can cloud judgment and background information that is needed for thorough evaluation.

The need for background information becomes apparent when one considers that focused and, at times, mildly leading questions are necessary with young children. Interviewers cannot formulate such questions without background information. Unlike an adult or adolescent rape victim, who comprehends the purpose of the interview, and who understands the meaning of a question such as Did anything happen? a young child may not understand the purpose of the interview or the topic of discussion until it is introduced by the interviewer. In short, interviewers perform more effectively when they are armed with background information.

Although an interviewer usually needs background information before an interview begins, he or she should not give the child the impression that the interviewer already knows what happened. For example, the interviewer should not say, "You can tell me about it, I know who hurt you." Research indicates that a child who believes the interviewer already knows what happened may be at increased risk of providing inaccurate information in response to focused or mildly leading questions (Warren et al., 1991).

Maintaining an open mind is critically important (White & Quinn, 1988). One of the most serious mistakes an interviewer can make is to reach a conclusion *before* the interview begins. Going into an interview with his or her mind already made up tempts the interviewer to adopt the theory that anything is legitimate that "helps the child disclose." This theory is defective. The purpose of the interview is *not* to confirm a prior finding of abuse, but to discover *whether* abuse occurred. An interviewer who begins the interview with the unshakable belief that abuse occurred cannot keep an open mind. The interviewer is likely to ignore evidence pointing away from abuse and overvalue evidence pointing toward it (Kendall-Tackett, 1991). The interviewer whose mind is already made up is prone to use highly leading questions and techniques that manipulate and even coerce children into agreeing with the interviewer's preconception of events.

Obviously, the open-minded interviewer cannot accept at face value a child's statement that "nothing happened." Many sexually abused children deny their abuse, especially at first (Sorensen & Snow, 1991; Summit, 1983). Furthermore, many abused children recant. The interviewer faces a difficult dilemma: How far should the interviewer push a child who says that nothing happened? There is no easy answer to this dilemma, although several factors are useful in decision making:

1. The stronger the evidence of abuse from sources other than the child, the greater the justification for pushing for disclosure, including, when necessary, mildly leading questions.
2. Reliable evidence that the child was threatened or coerced into silence may justify greater probing.
3. The exigencies of the case are important. If a child's immediate safety is at stake, the interviewer may have little choice but to press for information. On the other hand, if the child is safe, the interviewer may terminate the interview after moderate probing and schedule a follow-up interview when the child may feel more comfortable disclosing.

ANATOMICAL DOLLS

Anatomical dolls are used during interviews by CPS professionals, law enforcement officers, mental health professionals, health care providers, and others (Boat & Everson, 1988; Conte, Sorenson, Fogarty, & Dalla Rosa, 1991). These dolls have two primary uses during interviews. First, they are used to help children communicate more effectively, much as a child might use toy cars to describe an auto accident. Second, apart from helping children communicate, a child's interaction with the dolls may supply evidence of abuse.

For example, a child's positioning dolls in sexually explicit poses may help the professional reach a conclusion about abuse.

Using a child's interaction with anatomical dolls as evidence of abuse is controversial. Existing research supports several conclusions. It is clear the dolls are not a test for sexual abuse (Everson & Boat, 1990); that is, a decision about sexual abuse cannot be based solely on a child's interaction with the dolls.

Explicit sexual positioning of dolls is not common among nonabused children, although a small percentage of nonabused children place dolls in what appear to be sexual positions, including positions suggestive of sexual intercourse and other sex acts (Everson & Boat, 1990). When a young child's use of dolls indicates detailed knowledge of the mechanics of sexual acts, the likelihood of sexual abuse increases, and further investigation is warranted.

When anatomical dolls are used properly—that is, nonsuggestively—they do not cause nonabused children to make false reports of sexual abuse. Goodman and Aman (1990) studied the effect of the dolls on the ability of 3- and 5-year-old children to recall a staged event. One week following the event, the children were interviewed. Some of the children were questioned with anatomical dolls. Suggestive questions were asked that might tempt children to make false reports of abuse. For example, children were asked, "He took your clothes off, didn't he?" and "He kissed you, didn't he?" Goodman and Aman conclude that "the use of anatomically detailed dolls in and of itself does not lead children to make false reports of abuse even under conditions of suggestive questioning" (p. 1870).

Everson and Boat (1990) summarize existing research, including their own, and conclude that the literature

> offers substantial evidence against the argument that anatomical dolls are too suggestive for use in sexual abuse evaluations with young children. In fact, there is little research support for the position that exposure to dolls with obvious sexual genitalia induces "normal" young children to fantasize about sex or to act out in their play in sexually explicit ways. (p. 741)

When children demonstrate what appear to be sexual behaviors with dolls, documentation is vitally important. A detailed record should be made of the child's interaction with the dolls, including the child's positioning of the dolls and any verbal, nonverbal, or affective responses, such as crying, anxiety, fear, anger, or regression. Careful documentation is essential regarding the spontaneity of the child's interaction with the dolls, and any indications the child possesses knowledge of sexual acts, anatomy, or vocabulary that one would not expect in a child of that age.

It is sometimes appropriate to limit use of anatomical dolls to helping a child communicate, and to avoid drawing conclusions about sexual abuse from the child's interaction with the dolls. When the use of dolls is limited in this way, the interviewer is not drawn into the debate about dolls as evidence of abuse. When dolls are used only to help a child communicate, this fact should be documented.

It is appropriate before an interview begins to inform an adult responsible for the child about the interview process, including the fact that anatomical dolls may be used. The adult may be informed that some children exhibit increased interest in their genitalia or in the genitalia of others following use of such dolls (Boat, Everson, & Holland, 1990). The adult may also be informed that exposure to anatomical dolls does not appear to cause sexual acting out or other inappropriate behavior.

Some preschool children, particularly 2- and 3-year-olds, may be distracted by the anatomical features of the dolls, and this distraction may interfere with their ability to remember and relate events (Goodman & Aman, 1990). If the interviewer believes the dolls are distracting a young child, they should not be used.

Use of anatomical dolls should normally be postponed until a child has a full opportunity to describe events verbally. However, there is no predetermined amount of time that must pass before dolls are introduced, nor is there any predetermined number or type of questions that should be asked beforehand. Every child is unique, and interviewers should use their discretion to determine when dolls will be useful.

Whether or not a child experiences difficulty communicating about sexual abuse, anatomical dolls are sometimes useful to confirm an interviewer's understanding of a child's verbal description of abuse, and to reduce the likelihood of miscommunication between the child and the interviewer. For example, some young children do not understand the term *private parts,* and point "to their ears, to their arms, and to other not-so-private places" when asked about them (Goodman & Aman, 1990; Goodman & Clarke-Stewart, 1991).

When a child provides a detailed verbal description of abuse, it may be wise for the interviewer to avoid using dolls. The use of dolls after a child has provided a verbal account of abuse may allow an attorney to argue that improper use of the dolls renders the child's description unreliable.

Boat and Everson (1988) offer useful guidelines for the use of anatomical dolls during interviews. The interviewer generally presents the child with a set of fully clothed dolls. The set normally includes adult and child dolls of both genders. The interviewer should avoid such expressions as "Let's pretend" and "Let's play," because these invite criticism. The interviewer may ask the child to select one of the dolls. Depending on the age and knowledge of the child, the interviewer may begin by asking the child to identify body parts on the fully clothed doll the child has selected. For example, the interviewer might point to the doll's eye and say, "What is this?" and "What does it do?" The doll is then undressed. The child may undress the doll. As the doll is undressed, the interviewer asks the child about body parts, including breasts and genitalia. If the child uses a childlike term to describe a body part, the interviewer asks questions to be sure he or she understands the child's meaning.

After the child's understanding of body parts is inventoried, and before questions are asked about sexual abuse, the child may be allowed a period of unsupervised free play with several dolls. If the child spontaneously engages in behavior that appears to be sexual, the behavior is carefully documented. It is often a good idea not to interrupt the child's sexualized behavior with the dolls. When the sexualized behavior stops, the interviewer may ask questions such as, "What were the dolls doing?" "Who is this?" "What is this doll's name?" "Did someone show the dolls how to do that?" "Who showed them?" If the child names a particular person, the interviewer clarifies the identity of the person to whom the child is referring.

When a child is questioned with the aid of dolls, the interviewer usually begins with nonfocused and nonleading questions designed to elicit spontaneous disclosure. If open-ended questions are not productive, focused questions are used. Highly focused questions, which may be leading, are avoided unless less directive questions are ineffective. It is not desirable for the interviewer to position dolls in sexually explicit positions and to ask the child to confirm whether "this is the way it happened."

SHOULD INTERVIEWS BE VIDEOTAPED?

One of the most controversial issues relating to interviewing is whether interviews should be videotaped. In some cities most interviews are videotaped, while in other cities few, if any, are taped. Critics of interview practices usually favor videotaping, arguing that unless an interview is on tape, the child's disclosure should be viewed with skepticism (Coleman & Clancy, 1990).

It is clear that videotaping is not a litmus test for reliability. The electronic hum of a video camera ensures neither honesty nor accuracy. This is not to say, however, that videotaping is irrelevant. No less an authority than the U.S. Supreme Court wrote that videotaping may increase confidence in a child's disclosure (*Idaho v. Wright*, 1990).

The recognition that videotaping is useful does not mean all interviews should be taped. The wide variety of circumstances in which children disclose sexual abuse often makes videotaping impractical. Many children disclose abuse to a parent. The realization that their child has been abused comes as a terrible shock to parents, and the first thought of many is to rush to the pediatrician, family doctor, or hospital emergency room. Thus, in many cases, physicians and nurses are the first professionals to interview sexually abused children. Such interviews often occur on an emergency basis in the doctor's office or hospital. In other cases, the first professionals to interview children are police officers or social workers. These professionals may talk to children at home, in the police car on the way to the hospital, at school, or at a children's shelter. In some cases, children disclose abuse during psychotherapy. In such cases, the therapist may have no advance notice of when the child will unlock the secret of abuse. Thus children disclose sexual abuse in a wide variety of settings and at unpredictable times. Seldom is a tape recorder or video camera available at the critical moment. Yet, children's statements during nonrecorded interviews are often highly reliable.

There is considerable disagreement on the wisdom of videotaping interviews. Some of the advantages and disadvantages of videotaping are outlined below.

Advantages

1. Videotaping may decrease the number of interviews. Other professionals can view the tape rather than reinterview the child.
2. Videotaping may lower the number of interviewers in the room with the child. Other professionals can watch the interview from another room or watch the tape when the interview is complete.
3. Videotaping documents exactly what was said by the child and by the interviewer. Taping also documents the child's affect and emotion, as well as details that may be forgotten as time passes.
4. When an interview is done properly, the existence of a videotape makes it very difficult to argue that the interviewer used improper questioning techniques.
5. Videotaping puts the interviewer in the spotlight, increasing the likelihood that he or she will use proper interview techniques and decreasing the temptation to hurry the child along or use questionable methods such as highly leading questions.
6. In some states a videotaped interview can be used in lieu of the child's testimony at subsequent legal proceedings.
7. The fact that a child's disclosure is on videotape may decrease the probability of recantation.
8. Viewing the videotape may convince the accused individual that the child will be a good witness and that the individual will be better off confessing.
9. A videotaped disclosure may be used to help persuade a skeptical nonoffending parent that abuse occurred.
10. Prior to trial, the prosecutor may use the videotape to refresh the child's memory about the abuse so the child will be a more effective witness in court.
11. An expert witness can use the videotape to help form an opinion about abuse. (See Chapter 5 for discussion of the types of information expert witnesses are allowed to use to reach conclusions about abuse.)

Disadvantages

1. The lawyer for the alleged perpetrator may concentrate the jury's attention on minor inconsistencies during the interview, or on

inconsistencies between the interview and the child's testimony in court. Such inconsistencies are inevitable. Nevertheless, the defense attorney may argue that inconsistencies render the child's testimony unreliable.

2. Because disclosure is a process, not an event, a single videotaped interview early in the investigation may provide an incomplete, inaccurate, and fragmented description of the abuse. Many abused children deny abuse during the initial interview. Other children are hesitant and halting, disclosing a little at a time. Disclosure may take several sessions. If the initial videotaped interview is viewed in isolation, the child may be unconvincing. The problem is compounded if subsequent interviews that provide the entire picture are not videotaped.

3. In many cases the videotaped interview is not the first disclosure. The initial disclosure may have been to a parent, teacher, or friend. The first disclosure may be highly trustworthy and probative of abuse despite the fact that it is not on tape. But the fact that the first disclosure is not taped means the initial disclosure may fall into the background as the videotaped interview takes center stage. Unfortunately, the videotaped interview may not be as convincing as the initial, unrecorded revelation.

4. If the interviewer asks so much as one questionable question, the defense attorney may argue that everything the child said is unreliable. The focus shifts away from what the child said, and onto the way the questions were asked. The defense attorney may exaggerate the negative impact of leading questions and other interview techniques.

5. It is impractical to videotape every contact with a child. If videotaping becomes the norm, however, children's statements that are not on tape may be viewed with increasing suspicion.

6. Videotaping makes some children (and some interviewers) nervous and uncomfortable.

7. In cases where the quality of the audio or video portion of the tape is poor, doubt may be cast on the entire interview.

8. Serious questions have arisen about the confidentiality of the videotapes. There is no way to guarantee such confidentiality. In many communities, judges enter protective orders that control access to videotapes (see the Appendix for a sample of such a court order). Illinois has a statute that makes certain misuses of such tapes a crime (see Illinois Annotated Statutes, Title 38, § 106A-4[c]).

Each community must work out its own approach to videotaping. There is no single right or wrong answer.

❏ Notes

1. Wakefield and Underwager's book, *Accusations of Child Sexual Abuse*, has been critically reviewed in Chadwick (1989), Myers (1990), and Salter (1991).

2. Sally's statement to her mother would be hearsay even if Sally *did* testify at trial. Thus if Sally testified, and said, "When I ran to my mom I said, 'Mommy, mommy, Bill played nasty with me. He put his finger in my pee-pee,' " Sally would be repeating her *own* hearsay statement. When Sally testifies and describes what Bill did to her, Sally's testimony is not hearsay. The hearsay rule is implicated only when a witness repeats a statement made at an earlier time.

3. Some aspects of the discussion of hearsay are simplified.

4. Virginia appears to be the only state in which the fresh complaint doctrine is limited to adult victims.

5. Technically, in most states a fresh complaint is not hearsay.

6. Some states do not have a hearsay exception for statements made for purposes of medical treatment or diagnosis. California, for example, has no such exception.

7. Not all states have a residual exception. For example, California lacks a residual exception.

3

Balancing the Need for Confidentiality and the Requirements of Disclosure

Abused and neglected children and their families interact with many professionals. For example, a sexually abused child might disclose to a teacher, who then reports to child protective services. A social worker interviews the child. The child visits a hospital for an examination and another set of questions. If mental health services are needed, the child sees a therapist. Members of the child's family are also involved with professionals. For example, an abusive or neglectful parent may seek psychotherapy. If legal proceedings are instituted in juvenile court, the judge may require parents to obtain counseling.

Each professional who interacts with an abused or neglected child or the child's family documents the interaction. It is not unusual for information about a family to be scattered through several agencies and offices. In the case described in the preceding paragraph, the teacher who first learned of the abuse made an entry in the child's school record. The CPS social worker opened a file and prepared a report. The doctor wrote a report too, which found its way into the hospital's medical records department. Each mental health professional serving the family had a file containing treatment information. Finally, a file was compiled at juvenile court. In some cases, the records can form a stack nearly as tall as the child. Needless to say, many of these records contain highly sensitive, private, and potentially embarrassing information that must be protected from inappropriate disclosure.

❑ Defining the Parameters of Confidentiality

The laws and ethical principles that protect confidential information disclosed to professionals safeguard the privacy of clients. To give maximum effect to the goal of protecting privacy, confidentiality should be defined broadly. Therefore, in this book *confidential information* is defined as any information shared between a client and a professional in the context of a professional relationship. A professional relationship exists whenever professional services are sought or provided, and includes consultation, diagnosis, testing, and therapy.

All information provided *by* the client should be considered confidential; this includes not only sensitive information that is obviously intended to be private, but also information such as the client's name and address. Confidentiality also includes information *about* the client that is obtained from other sources. Finally, information provided by the professional *to* the client is confidential. Thus the professional's comments to the client are as confidential as the client's comments to the professional.

The strongest case for confidentiality exists between a professional and a client receiving mental health or medical services. Confidentiality is less clear regarding information disclosed during investigative interviews conducted by CPS and law enforcement professionals. Even in investigative interviews, however, the norm should be protection of confidential information.

❑ **Sources of
Confidentiality and Privilege**

It is important to distinguish among three sources of confidentiality: (a) the broad ethical duty to protect confidential information, (b) laws making certain records confidential, and (c) privileges that apply in legal proceedings.

THE ETHICAL DUTY TO
SAFEGUARD CONFIDENTIAL INFORMATION

The ethical principles of social work, psychology, psychiatry, medicine, nursing, and related professions require professionals to safeguard confidential information revealed by clients. The Code of Ethics of the National Association of Social Workers (1980) states, "The social worker should respect the privacy of clients and hold in confidence all information obtained in the course of professional service." The ethical principles of the American Psychological Association (1981) state, "Psychologists have a primary obligation to respect the confidentiality of information obtained from persons in the course of their work as psychologists." The principles of medical ethics of the American Medical Association (1989) require physicians and psychiatrists to "safeguard patient confidences within the constraints of the law." The Hippocratic oath states that "whatsoever I shall see or hear in the course of my profession . . . if it be what should not be published abroad, I will never divulge, holding such things to be holy secrets." The ethics code of the American Nurses Association (1985) states that nurses are to safeguard the patient's right to privacy by carefully protecting information of a confidential nature.

It is clear that professionals have an ethical duty to protect confidential information disclosed during one-on-one professional relationships. Thus a client's statements to a psychotherapist must be protected from improper disclosure. The ethical duty also requires protection of confidential information disclosed during group therapy.

Difficult questions can arise when the client in therapy is a child. The ethical obligation to protect confidential information applies regardless of age, and confidential information cannot be revealed to outsiders unless

The ethical obligation to protect confidential information applies regardless of age.

consent is obtained. But are parents "outsiders"? May professionals discuss confidential information with parents and caretakers without the child's permission? A simple example illustrates why there is no across-the-board answer to this question. Suppose a professional's clients are 3 and 15 years of age. In the preschooler's case it is clear that the child's parents will be consulted regularly. The child may be informed that the therapist talks to "mommy" and "daddy," but it would be developmentally inappropriate to seek the child's "consent" to disclosure of information revealed during therapy. By contrast, it may be developmentally and therapeutically appropriate to safeguard the teenager's confidential revelations, even from parents (Nye, 1980, p. 282).

Regardless of the child's age, the professional's first duty is to the child (American Psychological Association, 1981). This is so regardless of who pays for therapy. Thus the fact that the 15-year-old's parents pay for the youngster's psychotherapy does not entitle the parents to confidential information. A useful way to deal with potential conflicts over access to confidential information is to set the ground rules before therapy begins. When the child is developmentally capable of participating in this process, the child's input should be obtained.

If a parent has abused or neglected a child, disclosure of confidential information to the maltreating parent may be contraindicated regardless of the child's age.

LAWS MAKING CLIENT RECORDS CONFIDENTIAL

Every state has laws that make certain records confidential. These laws define the circumstances in which confidential information may be disclosed. Some of the laws pertain to records compiled by government agencies such as CPS, schools, and the juvenile court. Other laws govern records created by professionals and institutions in the private sector such as physicians, psychotherapists, and private hospitals.

Statutes that make records confidential supplement the ethical obligation to safeguard private information about clients. Confidentiality laws and ethical obligations work in tandem to increase protection for confidential information about abused children and their families.

PRIVILEGED COMMUNICATIONS

The ethical duty to protect confidential information applies in *all* settings. Professionals are no less ethically bound to protect confidential information during casual dinner conversation than in the courtroom. In legal proceedings, however, certain professionals have an *additional* duty to protect confidential information. The law prohibits disclosure during legal proceedings of confidential communications between certain professionals and their clients. These laws are called *evidentiary privileges,* or *privileges* for short.

Unlike the across-the-board ethical obligation to protect confidential client information, privileges apply only in legal proceedings. Privileges clearly apply when professionals testify *in court* and are asked to reveal privileged information. Privileges also apply during legal proceedings outside the courtroom. For example, in most civil cases, and in some criminal cases as well, attorneys take pretrial depositions of potential witnesses. Depositions often occur at an attorney's office. The professional who is being deposed takes the oath that is administered to witnesses in court. The attorneys ask questions similar to the questions asked during trial. The deposition is recorded and transcribed by a court reporter. Following the deposition, the professional reads the transcription and certifies that it is accurate. If questions are asked during a deposition that call for privileged information, the professional or one of the attorneys should raise the privilege issue. More is said below about the role of the professional in asserting a privilege on behalf of a client.

Professionals should be sensitive to issues of confidentiality and privilege whenever they communicate with attorneys. It is usually good practice to decline communication regarding confidential information—whether in writing, over the phone, or in person—until the professional obtains consent from the client or, in the case of a child, the child's parent.

When is communication between a client and a professional privileged? Three requirements must be met. First, the communication must be between a client and a professional with whom privileged communication is possible. Not all professions are covered by privilege statutes. For example, most states have laws creating a privilege for confidential communications between certain psychotherapists and their clients. If the client talks to a psychotherapist who is not covered by the privilege law, no privilege applies. Of course, the fact that a privilege does not apply does nothing to undermine the therapist's ethical duty to protect confidential information. In legal proceedings, however, the presence or absence of a privilege makes an important difference. In court, a professional generally must answer questions that require disclosure of information the professional is ethically bound to protect. By contrast, the professional generally cannot be made to answer questions that require disclosure of privileged information. Thus, in legal proceedings, the existence of a privilege gives added protection to confidentiality—protection that is not available under the ethical duty.

The second requirement of privilege is that the client seek professional services. To continue the example of the psychotherapist, the client must consult with the therapist to obtain professional advice or therapy. If the client enters therapy, the privilege applies to confidential communications during therapy. Even though the client does not formally enter therapy, the privilege may apply to confidential communications between the client and the professional. For example, a client may consult a psychotherapist who refers the client to a second professional. In most states, communications between the client and the referring psychotherapist are privileged even though the client did not enter treatment with the referring professional.

Third, only communications that the client intends to be confidential are privileged. The privilege does not attach to communications that the client intends to be released to other people.

The fact that a third person is present when a client discloses information may or may not eliminate the confidentiality required for a privilege. The deciding factor is whether the third person is needed to assist the professional. For example, suppose a physician is conducting a physical examination and interview of a child. The presence of a nurse during the examination does not undermine the confidentiality of information revealed to the doctor. Furthermore, the presence of the child's parents need not defeat confidentiality. Again, the important factor is whether the third person is needed to help the professional do the job.

A privilege is not eliminated when professional colleagues consult about cases. According to Nye (1980):

> A patient's confidential data may be shared without his/her consent within the clinic/agency or institution for purposes of the patient's treatment. It is generally accepted that supervisors and consultants are considered part of the patient's "treatment team." Any such professional with whom information is shared will have the same duty to maintain confidentiality as the patient's own therapist. (pp. 281-282)

As discussed earlier in this chapter, the ethical duty to protect confidential information applies to information disclosed during group therapy. But do privileges apply when confidential information is shared during group, or does the presence of several people eliminate the possibility of privileged communication? The better approach to this issue is found in court decisions stating that privileges apply to group therapy (*Lovett v. Superior Court*, 1988).

Every state has a privilege for confidential communications between clients and attorneys. Most states also have some version of the following privileges:

1. client-physician privilege
2. client-psychotherapist privilege
3. confidential communications with members of the clergy

The client-psychotherapist privilege generally applies to psychiatrists and psychologists, but in many states it also includes clinical social workers, counselors, nurses, and other professionals providing psychotherapy.

Privileges available in a smaller number of states include the following:

1. sexual assault victim-counselor privilege
2. client-social worker privilege

A professional who wants to find out whether or not he or she is covered by a privilege should ask an attorney in his or her community or in the state professional organization.

Verbal communications are obviously covered by the privileges. So are gestures intended to communicate. Finally, confidential written communications are covered.

Privileged communications remain privileged when the relationship with the client ends. In most situations, the death of the client does not end the privilege.

The privilege belongs to the client, not the professional. In legal parlance, the client is the "holder" of the privilege.[1] As the privilege holder, the client can prevent the professional from disclosing privileged information in legal proceedings. For example, suppose a psychotherapist is subpoenaed to testify about a client. While the professional is on the witness stand, the attorney who subpoenaed the therapist asks questions that call for privileged information. At that point, the client's attorney should object. The client's attorney asserts the privilege on behalf of the privilege holder, the client. The judge then decides whether a privilege applies.

If the client's attorney fails to object to a question calling for privileged information, or if the client is not represented by an attorney, the professional may assert the privilege on behalf of the client. Indeed, the professional may have an ethical duty to assert the privilege if no one else does. The professional might turn to the judge and say, "Your honor, I would rather not answer that question because answering would require disclosure of information I believe is privileged." When the judge and attorneys learn that a privilege may exist, the legal professionals decide whether the question should be answered. In the process, the judge and the attorneys may question the professional to determine whether a privilege applies.

If the judge determines that a privilege applies, the professional will not have to answer the attorney's question. On the other hand, if the judge decides that no privilege applies, the judge will instruct the professional to answer. At that point the professional has to make a decision: either answer the question as instructed by the judge or continue to assert the client's privilege, and decline to answer. In most cases the professional obeys the judge's instruction and answers the question. The professional can hardly be criticized for following the judge's instruction. After all, the professional is in no position to second guess a judge's decision. In one last effort to avoid disclosing privileged information, the professional might, on rare occasions, inform the judge of the professional's dilemma and ask the judge's permission to consult an attorney before deciding whether to answer. Some judges will grant this request; others will not. In the end, if the professional declines to answer after being ordered by the judge to do so, the judge has several options. He or she may simply let the matter drop. More likely, the judge will order the professional's testimony up to that point stricken from the record and dismiss the professional as a witness. The judge has the authority to hold the professional in contempt of court for refusing to answer.

❑ Disclosure of Confidential and Privileged Information

The following subsections discuss disclosure of confidential and privileged information.

CLIENT CONSENT

Client consent plays the central role in release of confidential information (American Psychological Association, 1981). As Gutheil and Appelbaum (1982) observe, "with rare exceptions, identifiable data [about patients] can be transmitted to third parties only with the patient's explicit consent" (p. 5). A competent adult client may consent to release of information to third parties such as attorneys, courts, and anyone else selected by the client. The client's consent must be fully informed and voluntary. The professional should explain any disadvantages of disclosing confidential information. For example, the client may be told that release to most third persons waives any privilege that would apply.

A professional who discloses confidential information without client consent can be sued by the client. With an eye toward such lawsuits, Gutheil and Appelbaum (1982) offer the following advice:

> It is probably wise for therapists always to require the written consent of their patients before releasing information to third parties. Written consent is advisable for at least two reasons: (1) it makes clear to both parties involved that consent has, in fact, been given; (2) if the fact, nature or timing of the consent should ever be challenged, a documentary record exists. The consent should be made a part of the patient's permanent chart. (p. 6)

When the client is a child, parents have authority to make decisions about confidential and privileged information on the child (Nye, 1980, p. 282). When a parent is accused of abusing or neglecting a child, however, it may be inappropriate for the parent to make decisions regarding the child's confidential information. For example, a parent may attempt to hide pertinent information from the judge by asserting the child's privilege. Needless to say, judges are not sympathetic to such tactics. The South Dakota Supreme Court wrote that "the parents are the proper parties to assert the privilege for the [child] under normal circumstances, but when it is the conduct of those same parents that is in issue, it would be an anomalous result to allow them to exercise the privilege" (*In re D.K.*, 1976, p. 648). When there is a conflict between the interests of the child and the parents, the judge may allow someone else, such as a guardian *ad litem*, to make decisions about confidential and privileged information.

SUBPOENAS

When a person is accused of child abuse, prosecution may be commenced in criminal court. Juvenile court proceedings may be instituted if the alleged perpetrator is the child's parent. If the accused individual denies the abuse, the defense attorney prepares for trial. Naturally, defense counsel seeks all information that could exonerate the accused. In particular, defense counsel may seek access to confidential records about the child. To gain access, the attorney may subpoena the records. In addition to issuing a subpoena for the records, the attorney may issue a subpoena requiring the professional to testify.

A subpoena is a formidable-looking document. A typical subpoena begins with these words:

> The people of the State of California, to Jane Doe.
> GREETINGS: YOU ARE ORDERED TO APPEAR AS A WITNESS at the date, time, and place set forth below.

A subpoena is issued by a court at the request of an attorney. It bears the official seal of the court and is signed by a judge or court clerk. A subpoena usually arrives in the hand of a process server, who can get a professional's morning off to a rocky start with the words, "Good morning, I hereby serve you with a subpoena. Please sign here to acknowledge receipt." A subpoena is a command by a court, and thus cannot be ignored or dropped in the circular file. Disobedience of a subpoena is disobedience of a court order, and can be punished as contempt of court.

There are two basic types of subpoenas: (a) a subpoena that requires an individual to appear at a designated time and place to provide testimony, sometimes called a subpoena *ad testificandum*; and (b) a subpoena that requires a person to appear at a designated time and place and to bring records or documents designated in the subpoena, sometimes called a subpoena *duces tecum*.

It is important to know that a subpoena does not override privileges such as the client-psychotherapist privilege.

It is important to know that a subpoena does *not* override privileges such as the client-psychotherapist and client-physician privileges. The subpoena requires the professional to go to court, but it does not mean the professional has to disclose privileged information. The judge decides whether a privilege applies and whether the professional has to answer questions or release records.

Before responding to a subpoena, the professional should contact the client. The client may desire to release confidential or privileged information. If the client's decision is informed and voluntary, the professional may comply.

It is often useful—with the client's permission, of course—for the professional to communicate with the attorney seeking testimony or records. Unless the client consents, the professional should not disclose confidential or privileged information during such a conversation. In some cases, the conversation lets the attorney know the professional has nothing that can assist the attorney, and the attorney may withdraw the subpoena. Even if the attorney insists on compliance with the subpoena, the telephone conversation may clarify for the professional and the lawyer the limits of relevant information in the professional's possession. Furthermore, if the subpoena requires production of records, the professional may use the conversation to clarify exactly what documents the attorney wants.

If questions arise about the validity of a subpoena or how to respond to it, the professional should consult an attorney. Professionals in government agencies can consult a government attorney who represents the agency. Hospitals and some clinics have attorneys to advise on such matters. Professionals in private practice can contact attorneys who have represented them on other matters. State professional organizations may also have useful information about responding to subpoenas, although most state organizations do not provide legal advice. The one attorney who is *not* in a position to give objective advice is the attorney who issued the subpoena.

In some cases it is possible for an attorney to convince a judge to quash a subpoena—that is, declare the subpoena invalid. A subpoena may be quashed if it seeks privileged information, is unduly burdensome, or is not in proper form.

REVIEWING CLIENT RECORDS
PRIOR TO TESTIFYING

Prior to testifying in court, the professional may review a child's record to refresh his or her memory about the case. In some cases, the professional takes the child's file to court so the file can be used to answer specific questions. Professionals should know, however, that in some states the professional's use of a child's file to refresh memory may entitle the defense attorney to examine the file, including confidential information. This subject is discussed in Chapter 6.

EDUCATION RECORDS

Records maintained by schools contain confidential information about students (Code of Federal Regulations, Title 34, Part 99, 1990). Generally, schools must obtain parental consent before releasing such information to individuals outside the school system. Schools may release confidential information about students in response to a court order or subpoena. However, before school administrators comply with a court order or subpoena, they must make reasonable efforts to notify parents.

Sometimes schools must release student information on short notice because of an emergency. The law allows such release without advance parental consent.

CHILD ABUSE REPORTING LAWS

Child abuse reporting laws require professionals to report suspected child abuse and neglect to designated authorities. (See Chapter 4 for discussion of reporting laws.) The reporting requirement overrides the ethical duty to protect confidential client information. Furthermore, the reporting requirement overrides privileges for confidential communications between professionals and their clients.

To illustrate the effect of the reporting obligation on confidentiality, let us consider a case in which a mental health professional is treating an adolescent for depression. The professional is ethically obligated to protect confidential information about the adolescent. Furthermore, the client-psychotherapist privilege applies. During the fifth session, the adolescent unexpectedly discloses sexual abuse. The professional must report the disclosure. In filing the report, however, the professional need not disclose everything about the client. Disclosure can be limited to information required to comply with the reporting law. In other words, the reporting law does not completely abrogate the obligation to protect confidential information.

THE PSYCHOTHERAPIST'S DUTY TO WARN
POTENTIAL VICTIMS OF DANGEROUS CLIENTS

In 1974, the California Supreme Court became the first court to rule that a psychotherapist has a legal duty to warn the potential victim of a client who threatens the victim during therapy (*Tarasoff v. Regents of the University of California*, 1974). The duty to warn overcomes both the ethical duty to protect confidential information and the client-psychotherapist privilege. If the therapist fails to take reasonable steps to protect the victim, and the client carries out the threat, the victim can sue the therapist.

In the years since the *Tarasoff* decision, judges have grappled with the difficult question of when psychotherapists have a legal duty to warn potential victims. Unfortunately, the law in this area remains unsettled and confused (Felthous, 1989). Most courts conclude that a duty exists to warn potential victims, but courts have not achieved consensus on when the duty arises. Some courts construe the duty broadly, others narrowly. In 1985, California enacted a statute on the subject that limits the duty to warn to situations in which "the patient has communicated to the psychotherapist a serious threat of physical violence against a reasonably identifiable victim or victims" (California Civil Code § 43.92).

EMERGENCIES

In certain situations, a professional needs to release confidential information to protect a client who is self-dangerous. Gutheil and Appelbaum (1982) note:

> When, in an emergency situation, a patient refuses to give consent or cannot be located for consent, a therapist may sometimes disclose appropriate data in the patient's interest. The situations in which this might be thought to be the case are so numerous . . . that if the exception is not to swallow the rule, such action should be limited to situations in which the patient's immediate welfare is clearly at stake. (p. 8)

COURT-ORDERED PSYCHOLOGICAL EVALUATIONS

A juvenile or family court judge may order a parent to submit to a psychological evaluation that will be used to help the judge evaluate parenting ability. Since everyone knows at the outset that the professional's report will be shared with the judge and the attorneys, the obligation to protect confidential information is limited. Although the professional will protect confidential information as much as possible, and will obtain client consent before releasing information to individuals other than those mentioned in the judge's order, it is unlikely that the formal psychologist-client privilege will apply in this situation.

THE CLIENT-LITIGANT EXCEPTION TO PRIVILEGES

Privileges such as the client-physician and client-psychotherapist privileges do not apply when the client deliberately makes the client's physical or mental condition an issue in a lawsuit. To use a simple illustration, suppose an individual consults a physician for treatment of a broken leg suffered in an auto accident. Later, the patient sues the driver of the other car, and seeks to recover monetary damages for pain and suffering caused by the broken leg. The patient has made the broken leg an issue in the case. The driver of the other car has a right to subpoena the doctor and ask the doctor questions about the patient's broken leg. The patient cannot bar the doctor's testimony by asserting the client-physician privilege. By placing physical condition in issue, the patient waived any privilege.

The client-litigant exception to privileges sometimes arises in child abuse and neglect cases. For example, in some divorce cases, one spouse accuses the other of child abuse. The accusing spouse may subpoena privileged records on the accused spouse in the hope of finding information that could be used to prove the abuse. When litigation is commenced in juvenile court to determine whether parents abused or neglected their child, the government attorney may subpoena privileged records on the parents. Courts have reached differing conclusions on whether the client-litigant exception applies in these types of cases (Myers, 1992). The best advice for a professional who has received a subpoena for testimony or records is to seek legal advice before talking to the attorneys and before releasing confidential or privileged information.

THE CRIME-FRAUD EXCEPTION TO PRIVILEGES

The law does not allow an individual to consult a professional for the purpose of obtaining information that can be used to commit a crime in the future or to perpetrate a fraud. The crime-fraud exception to privilege is based on the realization that the policy of protecting confidential communications must not be used as "a cloak or shield for the perpetration of a crime or fraudulent wrongdoing" (*United States v. Gordon-Nikkar*, 1975).

❏ Note

1. In some states, and with some privileges, the professional is also a holder of a privilege. In California, for example, both the clergyperson and the layperson seeking spiritual advice are holders of the clergy-penitent privilege (California Evidence Code § 1034).

4

The Reporting Laws

In 1962, momentous steps were taken in the effort to protect children. In that year, Dr. C. Henry Kempe and his colleagues published their seminal article describing battered child syndrome (Kempe, Silverman, Steele, Droegmuller, & Silver, 1962), focusing national attention on the plight of abused children. That was also the year the Children's Bureau of the U.S. Department of Health, Education and Welfare sponsored an important conference on child abuse. The conferees recommended adoption of laws that would require professionals to report suspected child abuse and neglect to appropriate authorities. Beginning in 1963, state legislatures enacted reporting laws, and in the short span of four years, every state had reporting legislation on the books.

In the 30 years that have passed since enactment of the first child abuse reporting laws, a great deal has been learned about abuse and neglect. The reporting laws have played a key role in the accumulation of that knowledge. In particular, the reporting laws provide essential data on the prevalence of abuse and neglect. In 1962, before enactment of reporting laws, the American Humane Association conducted the first nationwide survey to estimate the prevalence of maltreatment. To gather data, the association was forced to turn to the only source of information available at the time—newspaper accounts! The survey revealed a total of 662 cases. With enactment of reporting laws, data emerged on the true prevalence of abuse and neglect. The reporting laws wrenched the secret of abuse and neglect out of the dark and into the light of day, where it could not be ignored.

Although the reporting laws provide valuable information on the incidence of child abuse and neglect, the laws serve a more immediate and important function. Simply put, reporting laws protect children. The reporting laws are an integral part of society's defense against child abuse and neglect. As legislators, admin-

> *The reporting laws are an integral part of society's defense against child abuse and neglect.*

istrators, and other concerned individuals grapple with the enigma of child maltreatment, one fact stands out: The reporting laws work. They are not perfect, but they serve an irreplaceable function, and they serve it well.

❑ Who Reports?

Professionals who work with children are required to report suspected abuse or neglect to designated child protection or law enforcement authorities. The list of mandated reporters includes educators, physicians, nurses, mental health professionals, social workers, and day-care providers. In the great majority of states, mandated reporters have no discretion as to whether or not to report. Reporting is mandatory, not optional.

❑ Definitions of Abuse and Neglect

Each state's reporting law provides definitions of physical abuse, sexual abuse, and neglect. Definitions vary slightly from state to state.

It is possible, however, to distill common themes from the various definitions. *Physical abuse* is defined as nonaccidental physical injury. *Sexual abuse* is often defined by reference to criminal laws on sexual abuse. *Neglect*, a broad concept that is difficult to define, generally includes failure by parents to provide minimally adequate food, clothing, shelter, education, or medical care. (See Chapter 5 for discussion of eight categories of neglect.)

❏ What Triggers a Report?

The reporting requirement is triggered when a professional possesses a prescribed level of suspicion that a child is abused or neglected. The terms used to describe the triggering level of suspicion vary slightly from state to state. These include "cause to believe," "reasonable cause to believe," "known or suspected abuse," and "observation or examination which discloses evidence of abuse." Despite shades of difference, the basic thrust of the reporting laws is the same across the country. Reporting is mandatory when a professional has evidence that would lead a competent professional to believe abuse or neglect is reasonably likely.

It is important to note that the duty to report does not require the professional to "know for sure" that abuse or neglect occurred. All that is required is information that raises a reasonable suspicion of maltreatment. A mandated reporter who postpones reporting until all doubt is eliminated probably violates the reporting law. The reporting law deliberately leaves the ultimate decision about whether abuse or neglect occurred to investigating officials, not to mandated reporters.

Uncertainty about when to report causes considerable anxiety. Fortunately, the law does not require professionals to be "right." Thus professionals do not violate the reporting law when they report suspected abuse that turns out not to exist. All the law requires is good faith and reasonable professional judgment. (See Chapter 7 for discussion of lawsuits against professionals who report suspected abuse or neglect.)

Zellman (1990), in a study of decision making among professionals required to report, gave professionals a set of carefully designed
vignettes and asked them whether they would file reports on each
one. Several factors influenced decision making. Not surprisingly,
seriousness of abuse played a key role in
the decision to report. Reporting behavior
was influenced by the professional's knowledge of the reporting law. Professionals in
Zellman's study were more likely to report
sexual abuse than physical abuse or neglect. The research also disclosed that de-

*Many professionals
fail to report abuse
and neglect that they
know about.*

cision making was influenced by the professional's belief that reporting would do more harm than good.

Many professionals fail to report abuse and neglect that they know
about (Zellman, 1990). As Finkelhor (1990) notes:

> A large proportion of serious abuse known to . . . professionals is not
> reported or identified by state child protection agencies. In 1986, only
> 40 percent of all maltreatment and 35 percent of the most serious cases
> known to professionals . . . were getting into the CPS system. There is
> an enormous reservoir of serious child abuse that CPS is still not
> discovering in spite of the increased reporting. (p. 25)

❏ Emergency Protective Custody

All states provide a mechanism to protect children in emergen-
cies. For example, in most states police officers have authority to
take children into temporary protective custody. Some states extend
this authority to CPS professionals and physicians. The law places
strict time limits on emergency protective custody, and if CPS workers want to keep a child in temporary custody for more than a short
time, they must commence proceedings in juvenile court.

❏ Photographs and X Rays Without Parental Consent

A substantial number of reporting laws authorize designated
professionals to take photographs or X rays of children who may be

abused or neglected. This authorization is important because children generally lack legal capacity to consent to such procedures. Parents have the authority to consent on behalf of their children. There is a remote possibility that a professional who takes pictures or X rays without parental consent could be sued. Obviously, in abuse and neglect cases, parents sometimes refuse to authorize photographs or X rays. In other cases, there is no time to contact parents for permission. In such cases, reporting laws in some states authorize necessary procedures without parental consent.

❑ Penalty for Failure to Report

Most reporting laws state that intentional failure to report suspected abuse or neglect is a misdemeanor. A small number of states (Arkansas, Colorado, Minnesota, Montana, New York) provide by statute that a person who fails to report can be sued for damages (see Myers & Peters, 1987, pp. 14-18).

❑ Immunity From Lawsuits

The reporting laws provide immunity from civil and criminal liability for professionals who report suspected abuse or neglect in good faith. The fact that the reporting law grants immunity does not mean a professional cannot be sued by an angry parent. Immunity means that if the professional is sued, he or she probably will not be held liable. (See Chapter 7 for discussion of lawsuits against professionals.)

❑ Duty to Report in Relation to Privileges and Ethical Duty to Protect Confidential Information

The reporting laws override the ethical duty to protect confidential information. The laws also override privileges, except the client-attorney privilege. Professionals must report suspected maltreatment despite the fact that they learn of the abuse or neglect through a confidential communication. The need to protect children is more important than the need to protect confidentiality. (See Chapter 3 for discussion of confidentiality.)

5

Expert Testimony
in Child Abuse
and Neglect Litigation

Child abuse and neglect are often difficult to prove in court. Maltreatment occurs in secret, and the child is usually the only eyewitness. Although many children are effective witnesses, some cannot testify. Most children who do testify find the courtroom a forbidding place, and when a child is asked to testify against a familiar person, even a parent, the experience can be overwhelming. Consequently, children's testimony is sometimes ineffective. The obstacles caused by ineffective testimony and lack of eyewitnesses are compounded by the paucity of physical evidence that is a common problem in maltreatment litigation, especially in sexual abuse cases (Bays & Chadwick, in press). Faced with a vacuum of evidence, attorneys frequently turn to medical and mental health professionals for expert testimony regarding abuse and neglect.

❏ **Defining Expert Testimony**

Litigation often involves technical, clinical, or scientific issues that are beyond the ken of the average juror.[1] When the jury needs help with technical, clinical, or scientific issues, the law turns to individuals with specialized knowledge. These individuals are called expert witnesses. It is easy to think of cases in which expert testimony may be needed. In a case involving the collapse of a bridge, an engineer helps the jury understand why the bridge fell. In another case, the issue may be whether a car's brakes failed because a mechanic installed them improperly, and the expert might be an experienced auto mechanic. In an auto accident case involving physical injury, a physician helps the jury understand the injury and the healing process. An expert, then, is a person with special knowledge, experience, or education who helps jurors understand technical, clinical, or scientific issues.

❏ **When Expert Testimony Is Allowed**

Expert testimony is allowed when specialized knowledge will help a jury decide a case (Federal Rules of Evidence 702). Clearly, if an issue is completely beyond the understanding of the jury, expert testimony is essential. For example, lay jurors lack the ability to interpret X rays, and must have the assistance of a physician. But an issue need not be completely beyond the understanding of jurors before expert testimony is permissible. In some cases, an expert adds depth to the jury's understanding of relatively familiar subjects. Everyone knows, for example, that constantly belittling a child can be harmful. An expert witness helps the jury understand the specific emotional consequences of psychological maltreatment. In some cases, expert testimony disabuses jurors of commonly held misconceptions about relatively common topics. For example, jurors may believe that a sexually abused child would quickly tell someone about the abuse. The expert helps the jury understand that many abused children delay reporting.

Expert testimony is appropriate on a broad range of subjects, from the arcane to the mundane. The important factor is not whether the issue is beyond the understanding of the jury, but whether the expert can help the jury come to the correct result.

❑ Who Qualifies to Testify as an Expert Witness

Before a person may testify as an expert witness, the judge must be convinced that the person possesses sufficient "knowledge, skill, experience, training, or education" to qualify as an expert (Federal Rules of Evidence 702). Normally, the proposed expert takes the witness stand and answers questions about his or her educational accomplishments, specialized training, and relevant experience. An expert on child abuse or neglect might be asked questions in the following areas:

- educational attainments
- specialized training in child abuse and neglect
- extent of experience with abused children
- familiarity with relevant professional literature
- membership in professional organizations and organizations focused on child maltreatment
- publications

A professional does not have to be a well-known authority to testify as an expert witness. For example, it is not required that the expert be a published author of books or articles. Nor do professionals necessarily need the letters M.D., Ph.D., or M.S.W. after their names. On some issues, a professional with a bachelor's degree and considerable experience is as much an expert as anyone else. The important factor is whether the jury will be helped by the professional's testimony (Wigmore, 1974).

Once the proposed expert's qualifications are described, the attorney representing the person against whom the expert's testimony will be used has the right to ask questions. The opposing attorney may try to convince the judge that the professional is not an expert and should not be permitted to testify as one. On the other hand, if the opposing attorney is satisfied that the professional is an expert, he or she may ask just a few questions, or none at all, at this preliminary stage.

At the end of the qualification process, the judge decides whether the professional may testify as an expert witness. If the professional qualifies as an expert, the attorney who asked the professional to testify begins questioning. This phase of the questioning is called direct examination. Following direct examination, the opposing attorney has the right to cross-examine the expert. Cross-examination can cause considerable anxiety; see Chapter 6 for a detailed discussion of this topic.

In physical abuse cases, expert testimony is usually provided by physicians. In some cases, a nurse, nurse practitioner, or physician's assistant could qualify as an expert on physical abuse.

In child sexual abuse cases, professionals from several disciplines possess expertise. It is important to emphasize that simply because a person holds a particular degree does not mean the person is qualified to testify as an expert on sexual abuse. Only a small fraction of social workers, psychologists, nurses, psychiatrists, and physicians are experts on this complex subject. Moreover, a professional qualified to provide one type of expert testimony on sexual abuse may not be qualified to provide other types of expert testimony on this subject. The expertise required to provide different types of expert testimony on child sexual abuse is discussed in more depth later in this chapter.

When it comes to neglect, some issues are the particular province of medical professionals. Expertise on other aspects of neglect is shared by medical and mental health professionals.

❏ The Form of Expert Testimony

Expert testimony usually takes one of three forms: an opinion, an answer to a hypothetical question, or a dissertation on a pertinent subject. The most common form of expert testimony is an opinion, although in sexual abuse cases, expert testimony frequently takes the form of a dissertation or lecture.

OPINION TESTIMONY

Expert witnesses are permitted to offer professional opinions. For example, in a physical abuse case, a physician could testify that, in his or her opinion, a child has battered child syndrome, and that the child's injuries are not accidental. In a neglect case, a psychologist could offer an opinion that a child's developmental delay is correlated with parental behavior.

The expert must be reasonably confident of the opinion. Lawyers and judges use the term *reasonable certainty* to describe the necessary degree of confidence. Unfortunately, the reasonable certainty standard is not self-defining, and the law does little to elucidate the term. It is clear that expert witnesses may not speculate or guess (Wigmore, 1974). It is equally clear that experts do not have to be completely certain before offering opinions (Louisell & Mueller, 1979). Thus the degree of certainty required for expert testimony lies between guesswork and absolute certainty. But locating reasonable certainty somewhere between the poles of guesswork and certainty adds little to the concept, and, in the end, the reasonable certainty standard fails to provide a meaningful tool to evaluate the usefulness of expert testimony.

A more productive approach to assessing the value of expert testimony looks beyond the rubric of reasonable certainty, and asks questions that shed light on the factual and logical strength of the expert's opinion. In formulating an opinion, did the expert consider all relevant facts? How much confidence can be placed in the accuracy of the facts underlying the expert's opinion? Did the expert have adequate understanding of pertinent clinical and scientific principles? Did the expert employ methods of assessment that are recognized as appropriate? Are the inferences drawn by the expert logical? Are the expert's assumptions reasonable? Is the expert reasonably objective? In the final analysis, the important question is whether the reasoning employed by the expert is logical, consistent, explainable, objective, and defensible. The value of the expert's opinion depends on the answers to these questions (Black, 1988; Rheingold, 1962).

When an expert offers an opinion, the testimony usually takes the following form:

Attorney: Do you have an opinion, based on a reasonable degree of clinical certainty,[2] about the cause of the child's injuries?

Expert: Yes, I have an opinion. [The expert does not give the opinion yet.]

Attorney: What is your opinion?

Expert: In my opinion, the child has battered child syndrome. The child's injuries probably are not the result of an accident.

In many states, the expert is allowed to begin with the opinion and follow with an explanation. Alternatively, the expert may begin by explaining the information that led to the opinion, and conclude with the opinion. Telling the jury about the information that forms the basis of the opinion gives the opinion meaning, and allows the jury to evaluate how much stock to place in the opinion.

THE HYPOTHETICAL QUESTION

In former days, expert testimony was often elicited in response to a hypothetical question asked by an attorney. A hypothetical question contains hypothetical facts that closely parallel the actual facts of the case. In a physical abuse case, the attorney might say, "Now, doctor, let me ask you to assume that all of the following facts are true." The attorney then goes on at some length describing injuries suffered by a hypothetical child. At the end, the attorney says, "Now, doctor, based on these hypothetical facts, do you have an opinion, based on a reasonable degree of medical certainty, whether the hypothetical child's injuries were accidental or nonaccidental?" The doctor gives an opinion about the hypothetical child's injuries. Armed with the expert's answer to the hypothetical question, the jury applies the expert's opinion to the real child.

The hypothetical question has long been criticized. Louisell and Mueller (1979) write that hypothetical questions "are generally at best an awkward means to get at the truth. They tend to be long, complicated, and difficult for all—judge, jury, counsel, witness—to understand. . . . such questions often distort the truth, misrepresenting or stifling the actual opinion of the expert" (p. 711). Experts generally do not like hypothetical questions because the attorney does most of the talking, and the expert is simply asked to confirm the story told by the lawyer.

Although hypothetical questions are useful in some situations, and are still common in some states, this cumbersome device is gradually falling out of favor.

EXPERT TESTIMONY
IN THE FORM OF A DISSERTATION

Rather than offer an opinion, an expert may testify in the form of "a dissertation or exposition of scientific or other principles relevant to the case, leaving to the [jury] to apply them to the facts" (Federal Rules of Evidence 702, Advisory Committee Note). This form of expert testimony plays an important role in child sexual abuse litigation. In the most common scenario, the defense attorney asserts that a child who delayed reporting or recanted should not be believed. In such cases, the expert provides the jury with a dissertation—or lecture, if you will—on the dynamics of sexual abuse, so the jury understands why children delay and recant.

In many cases, an expert witness offering a dissertation does not mention the child in the case at hand. Indeed, an expert who knows nothing about the child is often able to help the jury.

❏ The Degrees of Legal Proof

The law uses three degrees of proof. From most to least demanding, these are (a) proof beyond a reasonable doubt, (b) clear and convincing evidence, and (c) preponderance of the evidence. The degree of proof that applies in a particular type of litigation is based on considerations of public policy (*In re Winship*, 1970). The goal of all litigation is to resolve disputes justly and accurately. It is recognized, however, that the legal system, like all human endeavors, is prone to error, and that incorrect litigation decisions occur. The degree of proof required in a case depends on the extent to which society is willing to tolerate the possibility of erroneous decision. In criminal litigation, where the defendant's reputation, liberty, and even life are at stake, society tolerates the least likelihood of error. A person accused of committing a crime is entitled to a presumption of innocence, and conviction requires the most convincing degree of evidence, proof beyond a reasonable doubt (*In re Winship*, 1970). Public policy dictates erring on the side of acquittal rather than conviction. To repeat the time-honored maxim, "One would rather that twenty guilty persons should escape the punishment of death, than one innocent person should be executed" (Fortescue, 1660).

In civil litigation, the degree of proof is less demanding than in criminal cases. A party prevails in a civil case when the evidence preponderates to some degree in the party's favor. For example, in child custody litigation incident to divorce, the judge awards custody to the parent who proves that it is more likely than not that the child's best interests will be served by awarding custody to that parent.

In most states, the preponderance of the evidence standard of proof is used in juvenile court proceedings to protect abused and neglected children. In order to invoke the juvenile court's authority to protect a child, the state must prove abuse or neglect by a preponderance of the evidence. To put it another way, the state must prove that it is more likely than not that maltreatment occurred.

In a small number of civil cases, the consequences of erroneous decision are so serious that American law demands more than a preponderance of the evidence. In these cases an intermediate degree of proof, commonly called clear and convincing evidence, is used. For example, before a state may permanently sever the parent-child relationship, the state must prove the grounds for termination by clear and convincing evidence (*Santosky v. Kramer*, 1982).

It is tempting to compare the three degrees of proof with percentages. One might compare proof beyond a reasonable doubt to 95% certainty, preponderance to 51% certainty, and clear and convincing evidence to 75-80% certainty. Although such comparisons provide some insight into the degrees of proof, the comparison is not very helpful. The degrees of proof are simply too complex to yield to simple percentages.

Expert witnesses are sometimes asked to express the certainty of their professional opinions in terms of the legal degrees of proof. Such requests are inappropriate. The degrees of proof are purely legal constructs, foreign to the process of clinical decision making about abuse and neglect. Clinical and diagnostic decisions are not made on the basis of proof beyond a reasonable doubt or a preponderance of the evidence, and the law does not require an expert's confidence in an opinion to vary with the type of litigation, or to mirror the degree of proof employed in a particular case. An expert testifying in a criminal case need have no greater confidence in an opinion than an expert testifying in a civil case. This is not to say that the expert's degree of certainty is irrelevant, and attorneys may be expected to inquire about the certainty of the opinion. The point is that expert witnesses need not conform their clinical decision making to the language of the law. Rather, the expert should state that the opinion is based on reasonable certainty, as that term is defined above.

❏ **Types of Information on Which Expert Witnesses May Base Opinions**

In their professional lives outside the courtroom, professionals draw from many sources of information to reach conclusions about abuse and neglect. When it comes to expert testimony, the law generally allows professionals to base opinions on the same sources of information they rely on in their normal, day-to-day practices. Thus in a sexual abuse case an expert witness may base an opinion to be offered in court on the child's disclosure, the results of a CPS investigation, and consultation with colleagues. In a physical abuse case, the physician may form an opinion on the basis of an interview and physical examination of the child, statements of the parents, results of laboratory tests and X rays, and readings in the professional literature.

In most states, expert witnesses are allowed to base opinions they offer in court on information that normally could *not* be used in court. Thus, in formulating an opinion, an expert may rely on information that the prosecutor would not be allowed to use as evidence. To put it another way, an expert's opinion may be *admissible* even though it is based partly on *inadmissible* information. The only limit on the expert's reliance on inadmissible information is that the information must be of the type generally used by professionals who make clinical and treatment decisions.

The potentially inadmissible information on which experts rely most frequently is written and verbal hearsay. (See Chapter 2 for discussion of hearsay.) Common examples of written hearsay include medical records, X-ray reports, and CPS reports. The most obvious verbal hearsay is the child's description of abuse. Oral statements by parents and others also play a role in forming the expert's opinion. Even though some of the written and verbal hearsay considered by the expert could not be used in court, the law allows the expert to rely on the hearsay to reach an opinion (*Broderick v. King's Way Assembly of God Church*, 1991).

After an expert offers an opinion, he or she usually goes on to describe the information on which the opinion is based. In doing so, the expert is usually permitted to describe all the information, including information that could not otherwise be used in court. In some cases, however, the judge instructs the expert to refrain from mentioning certain items of inadmissible information that the judge does not want the jury to hear.

Expert witnesses should be forthcoming about uncertainties and weaknesses that may undermine the strength of their conclusions. Equally important, experts should acknowledge the limits of their expertise, and should decline to exceed those limits, even under pressure from attorneys and judges to do so (Melton & Limber, 1989).

❑ Expert Testimony on Ultimate Factual and Legal Issues

In all types of litigation, issues of "ultimate" fact and law are decided. In child abuse and neglect litigation, the ultimate factual issue is whether the child was abused or neglected. The ultimate legal issue in a criminal case is guilt or innocence. In juvenile court, the ultimate legal issue is whether the juvenile court has authority to protect the child.

Expert witnesses are not allowed to offer opinions on ultimate *legal* issues such as guilt or juvenile court authority. Thus, in a criminal case, an expert should not say, "In my opinion, the defendant committed the crime." In a juvenile court case, an expert should not say, "In my opinion, the court should adjudicate the child a ward of the court." As Melton et al. (1987) note, professionals "should refrain from giving opinions as to ultimate legal issues. . . . Ultimate legal issues are issues of social and moral policy, and they properly lie outside the province of scientific inquiry" (p. 14).

Although expert witnesses must refrain from opinions on ultimate *legal* issues, the law in most states allows experts to offer opinions on ultimate *factual* issues. In particular, experts generally are permitted to offer opinions on whether a particular condition existed (Federal Rules of Evidence 704(a)). In child abuse and neglect litigation, it is important to determine whether an expert opinion that a child was neglected or abused is an opinion of ultimate fact (permissible) or an opinion of law (impermissible).

In physical abuse litigation, expert testimony is factual, and the debate about expert testimony on legal issues seldom arises. A physician who testifies that a child has battered child syndrome provides an opinion of fact, not law. Similarly, testimony that a child died from nonaccidental injuries is factual. The doctor is not offering an opinion about someone's guilt or innocence.

In child sexual abuse litigation, there is disagreement over whether mental health professionals should be allowed to give an opinion that a child was sexually abused. Some commentators take the position that an opinion that sexual abuse occurred is a factual conclusion, not an impermissible opinion on legal issues (Myers, 1992; Myers et al., 1989). Professionals routinely use clinical judgment to reach conclusions about sexual abuse, and in doing so they reach factual, not legal, conclusions. Thus, when a mental health professional testifies that a child was sexually abused, the professional offers an opinion of fact, not an opinion on whether the defendant should be convicted or the juvenile court should assume jurisdiction. Not all commentators agree, however. Melton and Limber (1989) argue that an opinion from a mental health professional that sexual abuse occurred is essentially a legal conclusion, and should not be allowed.

In neglect cases, expert witnesses usually are not asked to offer an opinion on whether a child is neglected. Rather, the expert is asked to describe the psychological, social, or medical effects of adult behavior toward children. This kind of testimony is factual and entirely proper.

□ **Expert Testimony in Physical Abuse Cases**

When physical abuse is charged, the accused individual may be guilty or innocent. An individual who denies responsibility usually uses one of two defenses. The most common defense is that the child's injuries were accidental. Alternatively, the individual may acknowledge that the child was abused, but claim that someone else is the abuser. Thus the attorney trying to prove physical abuse may have to prove two things: (a) that the child's injuries were not accidental, and (b) that the accused person is the one who inflicted the injuries.

Expert testimony from medical professionals plays a key role in proving nonaccidental injury (Chadwick, 1990). Physicians regularly provide testimony about bruises, bites, head injuries, abdominal injuries, burns, and fractures (Schmitt, 1987).

MEDICAL TESTIMONY DESCRIBING SYNDROMES

Physicians often describe syndromes that indicate nonaccidental injury, such as the following.

Battered Child Syndrome

In the now famous article in which Kempe and his colleagues (1962) coined the term *battered child syndrome*, the authors describe the syndrome as follows:

The battered child syndrome may occur at any age, but, in general the affected children are younger than 3 years. In some instances the clinical manifestations are limited to those resulting from a single episode of trauma, but more often the child's general health is below par, and he shows evidence of neglect including poor skin hygiene, multiple soft tissue injuries, and malnutrition. One often obtains a history of previous episodes suggestive of parental neglect or trauma. A marked discrepancy between clinical findings and historical data as supplied by the parents is a major diagnostic feature of the battered-child syndrome. . . . Subdural hematoma, with or without fracture of the skull . . . is an extremely frequent finding even in the absence of fractures of the long bones. . . . The characteristic distribution of these multiple fractures and the observation that the lesions are in different stages of healing are of additional value in making the diagnosis. (p. 17)

Judges routinely allow physicians to testify that a child has battered child syndrome, and that the child's injuries are probably not accidental (Myers, 1992). In addition to allowing statements that a child's injuries are nonaccidental, judges allow physicians to describe the means used to inflict injuries. For example, a doctor could state that a skull fracture was probably caused by a blow from a blunt instrument such as a fist. Judges generally allow medical experts to state whether the caretakers' explanation for the child's injuries is reasonable.

Not all victims with battered child syndrome have injuries in different stages of healing. Kempe et al. (1962) note that abusive injury sometimes results from "a single episode of trauma." Many child abuse fatalities lack a pattern of repeated injury. According to Zumwalt and Hirsch (1987), "Fatalities from an isolated or single beating are as common as fatalities from repeated physical assault" (p. 258).

Shaken Baby Syndrome

A young child can suffer serious neurological injury when shaken violently by an adult (Caffey, 1974; Dykes, 1986). The terms *shaken baby syndrome* and *whiplash shaken infant syndrome* are used to describe such injuries. Judges permit physicians to describe this syndrome and to offer an opinion that a child's injuries were probably caused by shaking (Myers, 1992).

Munchausen Syndrome by Proxy

Munchausen syndrome in adults is defined as "a condition characterized by habitual presentation for hospital treatment of an apparent acute illness, the patient giving a plausible and dramatic history, all of which is false" (*Dorland's Illustrated Medical Dictionary*, 1981, p. 1295). Munchausen syndrome by proxy occurs when an adult uses a child as the vehicle to present fabricated illness (Libow & Schreier, 1986; Mehl, Coble, & Johnson, 1990; Orenstein & Wasserman, 1986). As Zumwalt and Hirsch (1987) write, "Munchausen syndrome by proxy occurs when a parent or guardian falsifies a child's medical history or alters a child's laboratory test or actually causes an illness or injury in a child in order to gain medical attention for the child which may result in innumerable harmful hospital procedures" (p. 276).

Although Munchausen syndrome by proxy appears to be an uncommon form of child abuse, when it occurs, judges allow physicians to describe the syndrome and to state whether a child has it (*In re Colin R.*, 1985; *People v. Phillips*, 1981).

DOCUMENTING CARETAKERS' EXPLANATIONS FOR A CHILD'S INJURIES

When physical abuse is suspected, the professional pays close attention to the caretakers' explanation of the child's injuries (Schmitt, 1987). In particular, the professional should document the factors described below.

Unexplained Injury

Abusive caretakers sometimes deny any knowledge of how the child was injured. Of course, a nonabusive caretaker may not know how accidental injury occurred, but if abuse is suspected and a caretaker's lack of knowledge sounds suspicious, the professional should document why lack of knowledge is questionable.

Implausible Explanation

One of the strongest indicators of nonaccidental injury is an explanation that "is implausible and inconsistent with common sense and medical judgment" (Schmitt, 1987, p. 179). For example, care-takers may state that a minor accident caused major injury. Abusive caretakers may say that a child with a severe head injury fell from a couch or other piece of furniture onto the floor. Chadwick, Chin, Salerno, Landsverk, and Kitchen (1991) report that parents often attribute fatal head injuries to falls of less than 4 feet. Their research discloses, however, "that life-threatening injury requires at least a 15-foot fall. . . . Falls of less than 4 feet are often reported in association with children's head injuries that prove to be fatal, but such histories are inaccurate in all or most such cases" (p. 1355). Chadwick and Myers (1992) write that "the probability of a child's dying in a fall of less than ten feet is very small." Williams (1991) adds that "falls of less than 3 to 4 feet do not produce serious injuries" (p. 1350).

> *"The probability of a child's dying in a fall of less than ten feet is very small."*

In some cases, caretakers say that injury occurred when a child engaged in activity the child could not perform. For example, care-takers may say that a 4-month-old baby was burned when the child climbed onto a stove and turned on the burner.

An implausible explanation is important for diagnostic purposes because it helps confirm the diagnosis of nonaccidental injury. In addition to its medical value, an implausible explanation has *legal* significance. An implausible explanation may be used as evidence of guilt. In one case, the court wrote:

> A jury may consider and give weight to any false and improbable statements made by an accused in explaining suspicious circumstances. . . . When we consider the defendant's improbable statement in this case together with the nature of the injuries to the child, the medical opinion evidence, and the defendant's opportunity [to abuse the child], we are persuaded that, taken together, they are sufficient to constitute substantial evidence of guilt. (*Payne v. State*, 1987, pp. 236-237)

Inconsistent Explanations

When abuse is suspected and the child has more than one care-taker, each caretaker should be questioned apart from the other. Since abusive caretakers seldom disclose the real cause of the child's injuries, they have to invent excuses. When caretakers are questioned separately, their excuses may be inconsistent, and inconsistency may undercut both explanations.

Injuries Explained as Inflicted by a Sibling

Siblings certainly can hurt each other, sometimes seriously. When a caretaker asserts that a child's serious injuries were inflicted by a young sibling, however, further investigation is warranted.

Delay in Seeking Medical Care

Delay in obtaining medical care for serious or life-threatening injury may indicate abuse. It is important, of course, not to read too much into delay in obtaining medical care—innocent explanations are possible. Yet, a desire to avoid detection sometimes explains delay.

❏ Expert Testimony in Sexual Abuse Litigation

Expert testimony plays an important role in child sexual abuse litigation. Such testimony can be divided into two broad categories: expert testimony describing medical evidence of sexual abuse, such as genital injury and sexually transmitted disease (*People v. Mendibles*, 1988), and expert testimony regarding the psychological effects of sexual abuse.

When sexual abuse is suspected, children should be examined promptly by a medical professional with expertise in child sexual abuse (Bays & Chadwick, in press). Although medical evidence may not be found, when it is, such evidence is allowed in court. An added benefit of the child's interaction with medical professionals is the opportunity to dispel the misconception shared by many children that they are "damaged goods." Doctors and nurses are in a unique position to reassure children that their bodies are normal.

Although some aspects of expert testimony from medical professionals are controversial, disagreement surrounding medical evidence pales in comparison to the debate swirling around expert testimony from mental health professionals. The remainder of this section grapples with the evolving subject of expert testimony from social workers, psychologists, psychiatrists, and related professionals.

Before reading on, however, the reader should answer a simple question. If you are a psychotherapist, do you need to know why a child is in your office before you begin treatment? The answer seems obvious. The answer is equally clear if your role is interviewing children to see if intervention is necessary. You have to decide whether abuse is likely. Whether you are a clinician or an investigator, you reach a conclusion based on all the information at your disposal. You are never 100% certain, but treatment and intervention decisions have to be made, so you gather as much information as possible, and you come to a professional judgment. The bottom line is that you decide whether or not abuse occurred.

In reading the following material about expert testimony, it is useful to keep in mind the decisions one makes *outside* the courtroom. When professionals don the mantle of expert witness, they may find that judges do not always allow them to describe some of the decisions they make every day in their nontestifying professional lives.

Expert testimony regarding the psychological effects of sexual abuse falls into two categories: (a) expert testimony offered as direct evidence of sexual abuse (e.g., an opinion that a child was abused); and (b) expert testimony offered for the more limited purpose of rehabilitating a child's credibility after that credibility has been attacked by the defense attorney (e.g., expert testimony that many abused children delay reporting abuse).

Professionals with relatively little experience and training can provide expert testimony to rehabilitate a child's credibility. In many cases, for example, rehabilitation testimony is limited to explaining that many sexually abused children recant or delay reporting. The expert does not venture an opinion that the child in the case at hand was abused. Indeed, in rehabilitation testimony it is often unnecessary to refer to the child. Rehabilitation testimony is straightforward and simple. To provide such testimony, the only requirement is knowledge of relevant literature. Thus a CPS social worker with six months on the job and knowledge of three or four pertinent articles is qualified to provide rehabilitation testimony on recantation and delayed reporting.

Contrast the limited expertise required for rehabilitation testimony with the extraordinary expertise required to formulate a diagnostic opinion that a child was sexually abused (American Professional Society on the Abuse of Children, 1990). Only a small fraction of professionals working with sexually abused children are qualified to provide such an opinion. The social worker described above, although qualified to offer rehabilitation testimony, is not qualified to offer an opinion that a child was sexually abused.

It is important not to lose sight of the different levels of expertise required for a professional to provide (a) expert testimony that a child was sexually abused and (b) expert testimony limited to rehabilitation of a child's credibility.

MENTAL HEALTH TESTIMONY
THAT A CHILD WAS SEXUALLY ABUSED

As mentioned previously, there is controversy over whether mental health professionals should testify that children have been sexually abused. Melton and Limber (1989) articulate a minority position when they write that "under no circumstances should a court admit the opinion of an expert about whether a particular child has been abused" (p. 1230). The majority of professionals believe qualified mental health professionals can determine whether abuse occurred; not in all cases, but in some. The majority position is reflected in guidelines published by the American Academy of Child and Adolescent Psychiatry (1988, 1990), which state:

> The effects of child sexual abuse are diagnosable in the same sense that other medical conditions are diagnosable—on the basis of history, physical examination and the judicious use of various tests. Rarely is one finding alone diagnostic of sexual abuse; rather, findings must be interpreted within the total context of a thorough evaluation. (1988, p. 657)

Most literature on child sexual abuse echoes the position of the American Academy of Child and Adolescent Psychiatry (Corwin,

1988; Faller, 1988; Faller & Corwin, in press; Myers et al., 1989). Sgroi, Porter, and Blick (1982) write that "most cases can be validated by investigative interviewing and by assessing the credibility of the history of sexual abuse elicited from the child" (p. 72). Faller (1990) observes that "there appears to be a fair amount of consensus among mental health professionals about both the strategy and the criteria for deciding whether a child has been sexually victimized" (p. 115). In 1990, the American Professional Society on the Abuse of Children issued guidelines for psychosocial evaluation of sexual abuse in young children. The guidelines state:

> Sexual abuse is known to produce both acute and long-term negative psychological effects requiring therapeutic intervention. Psychosocial assessments are a systematic process of gathering information and forming professional opinions about the source of statements, behavior, and other evidence that form the basis of concern about possible sexual abuse. Psychosocial evaluations are broadly concerned with understanding developmental, familial, and historical factors and events that may be associated with psychological adjustment. The results of such evaluations may be used to assist in legal decision making and in directing treatment planning.

Assessing children for possible sexual abuse is a complex task requiring skill and experience. The professional must possess specialized knowledge of child development, individual and family dynamics, patterns of child sexual abuse, the disclosure process, signs and symptoms of abuse, and the uses and limits of psychological tests. The professional is familiar with the literature on child abuse, and understands the significance of developmentally inappropriate sexual knowledge. The professional is trained in the art of interviewing children. The professional is aware of the literature on coached and fabricated allegations of abuse. Of tremendous importance is the professional's understanding of sexually abused and nonabused children. Depth of understanding provides the reference point against which new cases are assessed. The combination of these specialized skills allows professionals to balance the multitude of factors involved in assessing suspected abuse.

Significance of
Symptoms Commonly Observed
in Sexually Abused Children

Among the many factors considered in evaluating possible sexual abuse, professionals pay close attention to the behavioral, emotional, and cognitive reactions observed in many sexually abused children. There is no single reaction observed in all sexually abused children. Moreover, reactions vary considerably. Nevertheless, the presence of commonly observed symptoms often provides evidence of abuse.

Many psychological symptoms are observed in sexually abused children. Symptoms of anxiety are particularly common, including fear, sleep disturbance and nightmares, flashbacks, startle reactions, hypervigilance, regression, bed-wetting, phobic behavior, withdrawal from usual activities, nervousness, and clingyness (Browne & Finkelhor, 1986; Mannarino & Cohen, 1986). Some sexually abused children are depressed (Lanktree, Briere, & Zaidi, 1991; Lipovsky, Saunders, & Murphy, 1989; Wozencraft, Wagner, & Pellegrin, 1991).

Examination of the foregoing symptoms reveals that they are associated with a number of traumatic events that have nothing to do with sexual abuse. For example, the fact that a child has nightmares and regression says little about sexual abuse. Other circumstances cause such symptoms. In fact, a child with nightmares and regression is more likely to be nonabused than abused. This conclusion is based on the base rate at which nightmares and regression occur in the population of children (Melton & Limber, 1989). To understand the base rate, consider the total population of nonabused American children. A small percentage of nonabused children have nightmares and regression. For purposes of illustration, suppose there are 30 million nonabused children, 5% of whom have nightmares and regression. Thus, in the population of nonabused children, 150,000 have nightmares and regression. Now consider the population of sexually abused children. Assume there are 300,000 sexually abused children, and that 10% of them have nightmares and regression. Thus, in the population of sexually abused children, 30,000 have nightmares and regression. If a child with nightmares and regression is selected at random, the odds are the child will be drawn from the much larger pool of *nonabused* children.

The base rate phenomenon is complex. Melton and Limber (1989) observe that "even psychologists who have had substantial statistical training often fail to appreciate the significance of base rates" (p. 1229). Clearly, professionals cannot base decisions about sexual abuse primarily on symptoms shared by abused and nonabused children.

> *Professionals cannot base decisions about sexual abuse primarily on symptoms shared by abused and nonabused children.*

Although many symptoms observed in sexually abused children are found in nonabused children, some symptoms are more strongly associated with personal or vicarious sexual experience. Examples of symptoms that have a closer connection to sexual abuse include developmentally unusual knowledge of sexual acts and sexualized play in young children (Beitchman, Zucker, Hood, DaCosta, & Akman, 1991; Friedrich, in press; Friedrich & Grambach, in press; Kolko & Moser, 1988; Mannarino & Cohen, 1986).

Friedrich, Grambach, Broughton, Kruper, and Beilke (1991) gathered data on sexual behavior in children who are not sexually abused. They write:

> A relatively clear finding is that despite the fact that 2- through 12-year-old children exhibit a wide variety of sexual behaviors at relatively high frequencies, e.g., self-stimulatory behavior and exhibitionism, there are a number of behaviors that are quite unusual. . . . These tend to be those behaviors that are either more aggressive or more imitative of adult sexual behavior. (p. 462)

In Friedrich et al.'s study, the sexual behaviors observed *least* often in nonabused children were placing the child's mouth on a sex part, asking to engage in sex acts, masturbating with an object, inserting objects in the vagina/anus, imitating intercourse, making sexual sounds, French kissing, undressing other people, asking to watch sexually explicit television, and imitating sexual behavior with dolls. The fact that a child demonstrates one or more of these uncommon sexual behaviors is not conclusive evidence of sexual abuse. Friedrich et al. state that "sexual behavior in children is related to the child's family context, most specifically the sexual behavior in the family" (p. 462).

Conte et al. (1991) surveyed 212 professionals who regularly evaluate children for possible sexual abuse. They asked the evaluators to rank the importance of 41 indicators used to assess sexual abuse. The following indicators were thought important by more than 90% of the evaluators: medical evidence of abuse, age-inappropriate sexual knowledge, sexualized play during the interview, precocious or seductive behavior, excessive masturbation, child's description consistent over time, and child's description reveals pressure or coercion.

Conte et al. say that "there are essentially many areas of agreement among the professionals in this sample" (p. 433). The researchers caution against placing undue confidence in their findings, saying that consensus among professionals "does not ensure that professional practice or professional beliefs are knowledge-based, and agreement among these respondents should not be assumed to validate various practices as reliable and effective" (p. 433).

Although current research has limitations, the findings of Friedrich et al., Conte et al., and others lend empirical support to the conclusion that presence in a child of sexual behaviors that are seldom observed in nonabused children supplies evidence of sexual abuse.

The diagnostic importance of symptoms observed in sexually abused children is highest when there is a coalescence of three symptoms: (a) a central core of sexual symptoms that are strongly associated with sexual abuse, (b) nonsexual symptoms that are commonly observed in sexually abused children, and (c) medical evidence of sexual abuse. Diagnostic importance declines as sexual symptoms and medical evidence decrease in proportion to nonsexual symptoms. When the only evidence consists of a number of ambiguous, nonsexual symptoms, the child's symptoms have little diagnostic value because of the base rate phenomenon.

Psychological Syndromes

Two psychological syndromes that play a role in child sexual abuse litigation are child sexual abuse accommodation syndrome and rape trauma syndrome, which are discussed in turn below.

Child sexual abuse accommodation syndrome. In 1983, Summit described child sexual abuse accommodation syndrome (CSAAS), naming five characteristics commonly observed in sexually abused children: (a) secrecy; (b) helplessness; (c) entrapment and accommodation; (d) delayed, conflicted, and unconvincing disclosure; and (e) retraction. Summit's purpose in describing the accommodation syndrome was to provide a "common language" for professionals working to protect sexually abused children. Summit did not intend the accommodation syndrome as a diagnostic device. Summit has observed that "the accommodation syndrome is neither an illness nor a diagnosis, and it can't be used to measure whether or not a child has been sexually abused" (quoted in Meinig, 1991, p. 6). The accommodation syndrome does *not* detect sexual abuse. Rather, CSAAS assumes that abuse occurred, and explains the child's reactions to it. Thus CSAAS is not the sexual abuse analogue of battered child syndrome, which *is* diagnostic of physical abuse. With battered child syndrome, one reasons from type of injury to cause of injury. Thus battered child syndrome helps diagnose physical abuse. With CSAAS, by contrast, one reasons from presence of sexual abuse to reactions to sexual abuse. Thus the accommodation syndrome does not prove abuse.

The accommodation syndrome has a place in the courtroom. The syndrome helps explain why many sexually abused children delay reporting their abuse, and why many abused children recant allegations of abuse and deny that anything happened. When the syndrome is confined to these rehabilitative purposes, the accommodation syndrome serves a useful forensic function.

Rape trauma syndrome. Rape trauma syndrome (RTS) was described by Burgess and Holmstrom in 1974 as "the acute phase and long-term reorganization process that occurs as a result of forcible rape or attempted forcible rape. This syndrome of behavioral, somatic, and psychological reactions is an acute stress reaction to a life-threatening situation" (p. 982). In *People v. Taylor* (1990), the New York Court of Appeals described RTS:

> According to Burgess and Holmstrom, the rape victim will go through an acute phase immediately following the incident. The behavior

exhibited by a rape victim after the attack can vary. While some women will express their fear, anger, and anxiety openly, an equal number of women will appear controlled, calm, and subdued. Women in the acute phase will also experience a number of physical reactions. These reactions include the actual physical trauma that resulted from the attack, muscle tension that could manifest itself in tension headaches, fatigue, or disturbed sleep patterns, gastrointestinal irritability and genitourinary disturbance. Emotional reactions in the acute phase generally take the form of fear, humiliation, embarrassment, fear of violence and death, and self-blame.

As part of the long-term reorganizational phase, the victim will often decide to make a change in her life, such as a change of residence. At this point, the woman will often turn to her family for support. Other symptoms that are seen in this phase are the occurrence of nightmares and the development of phobias that relate to the circumstances of the rape. For instance, women attacked in their beds will often develop a fear of being indoors, while women attacked on the street will develop a fear of being outdoors. (p. 134)

The third revised edition of the American Psychiatric Association's (1987) *Diagnostic and Statistical Manual of Mental Disorders* (DSM-III-R) lists rape among the stressors that can cause post-traumatic stress disorder (p. 248).

Although expert testimony on RTS is used most often in litigation involving adult victims, RTS is a useful concept in child sexual abuse litigation involving older children and adolescents. Expert testimony on RTS has been offered by prosecutors for two purposes: (a) to prove lack of consent to sexual relations and (b) to explain certain behaviors, such as delay in reporting rape, that jurors might misconstrue as evidence that rape did not occur.

Admissibility of RTS to prove lack of consent.[3] Courts are divided on the admissibility of RTS to prove lack of consent. Several courts reject RTS to prove lack of consent (*Commonwealth v. Gallagher*, 1988; *State v. Black*, 1987). In *People v. Taylor* (1990), the New York Court of Appeals wrote that "evidence of rape trauma syndrome does not by itself prove that the complainant was raped" (p. 135). The court concluded that "evidence of rape trauma syndrome is inadmissible when it inescapably bears solely on proving that a rape occurred" (p. 138). The California Supreme Court reached a similar result in

People v. Bledsoe (1984), where the court ruled that "expert testimony that a complaining witness suffers from rape trauma syndrome is not admissible to prove that the witness was raped" (p. 301).

Several courts have ruled that RTS is admissible when the defendant asserts that the woman consented (*State v. Allewalt*, 1986; *State v. Brodniak*, 1986; *State v. Huey*, 1985; *United States v. Carter*, 1988). In *State v. Marks* (1982), the Kansas Supreme Court stated that "when consent is the defense in a prosecution for rape qualified expert psychiatric testimony regarding the existence of 'rape trauma syndrome' is relevant and admissible" (p. 1294). In *State v. McCoy* (1988), the West Virginia Supreme Court of Appeals wrote, "We agree with the Supreme Court of Kansas that in a prosecution for rape where consent is the defense, qualified expert testimony regarding the existence of symptoms consistent with rape trauma syndrome is relevant and admissible" (pp. 736-737).

Courts that allow RTS to prove lack of consent place limits on the evidence. Thus courts do not permit expert witnesses to testify that the alleged victim was, in fact, raped. In *State v. McCoy* (1988), the court wrote, "The expert may testify that the alleged victim exhibits behavior consistent with rape trauma syndrome, but the expert may not give an opinion, expressly or implicitly, as to whether or not the alleged victim was raped" (p. 737).

Illinois has a statute stating that expert testimony "relating to any recognized and accepted form of post-traumatic stress syndrome shall be admissible as evidence" (Illinois Annotated Statutes, 1990). "The statute allows the admission of rape-trauma-syndrome testimony" (*People v. Harp*, 1990).

Admissibility of RTS to explain behavior that the jury might misconstrue as evidence that rape did not occur. Most courts allow expert testimony on rape trauma syndrome to rehabilitate the victim's credibility by explaining behaviors such as delay in reporting rape, which jurors might misconstrue as evidence that rape did not occur (*People v. Hampton*, 1987; *State v. Graham*, 1990). In *People v. Bledsoe* (1984), the California Supreme Court wrote, "Expert testimony on rape trauma syndrome may play a particularly useful role by disabusing the jury of some widely held misconceptions about rape and rape victims, so that it may evaluate the evidence free of the constraints of popular myths" (p. 457). In *People v. Taylor* (1990), the New York Court of Appeals approved expert testimony explaining why a rape victim might not appear upset following the assault. In *Commonwealth v. Mamay* (1990), a physician sexually assaulted several female patients. The Massachusetts Supreme Judicial Court approved expert testimony to explain why, "in the context of a trust relationship, some victims may return to the trusted relationship for further contact with the perpetrator of the assault" (p. 951).

Courts that allow RTS to explain behaviors observed in rape victims place limits on such evidence. Thus several court decisions state that the expert should describe behaviors observed in rape victims *as a group,* and should not refer to the victim in the case at hand (*People v. Coleman,* 1989). Some courts express concern that jurors will be confused by the term *rape trauma syndrome* (*State v. Gettier,* 1989).

Questionable Techniques for Assessing the Possibility of Child Sexual Abuse

Two additional techniques for evaluating children's descriptions of sexual abuse require mention. First, Gardner (1987a, 1987b, 1989) has described what he calls the Sex Abuse Legitimacy Scale (see also Moss, 1988). Expert witnesses occasionally rely on Gardner's scale to determine whether allegations of abuse are true. The Sex Abuse Legitimacy Scale has not been empirically validated, however, and is not generally accepted as reliable by experts on child sexual abuse (Berliner & Conte, in press).

The second technique worth mentioning has two components: statement validity analysis (SVA) and criterion-based content analysis (CBCA). CBCA entails analysis of a child's description of abuse in light of a specified set of criteria (Raskin & Esplin, 1991). SVA is the overall assessment of the likelihood of abuse. If future research supports the reliability of SVA and CBCA, these techniques may hold some promise for helping the assessment process. At the present time, however, SVA and CBCA have not found general acceptance in the scientific community. Wells and Loftus (1991) write:

> We have concerns about CBCA with regard to the adequacy of its current empirical support, the ability of the technique to partition

individual and age-related differences in linguistic abilities from va-
lidity-related differences, and the potential problem of overbelief of
the results of CBCA on the part of judges and juries. . . . Statements in
court to the effect that a particular child's statement is true or false are
not justified at this time. . . . Indeed, at this point we are not convinced
that CBCA would pass the Frye test of being generally accepted as
reliable and valid by the relevant community of scientists. (p. 171)

Position of the Courts on
Mental Health Testimony That
a Child Was Sexually Abused

Courts are divided on whether mental health professionals may
provide expert testimony that a child was sexually abused. One
group of courts allows properly qualified mental health professionals to testify that a child probably was sexually abused (e.g., *Broderick
v. Kings Way Assembly of God Church*, 1991 [Alaska]; *Glendening v. State*,
1987 [Florida]; *Seering v. Department of Social Services*, 1987 [Califor-
nia]; *Shannon v. State*, 1989 [Nevada]; *State v. Hester*, 1988 [Idaho]; *State
v. Charles*, 1990 [West Virginia]). A second group of courts rejects testimony from mental health professionals that abuse occurred (e.g.,
Johnson v. State, 1987 [Arkansas]; *Commonwealth v. Dunkle*, 1992 [Pen-
nsylvania]; *State v. Lamb*, 1988 [Wisconsin]; *State v. Schimpf*, 1989
[Tennessee]). Finally, a third group of courts adopts a middle position regarding testimony from mental health professionals that abuse
occurred. These courts state that such testimony may become admissible in the future if a strong showing is made that such testimony is reliable (e.g., *Goodson v. State*, 1990 [Mississippi]; *In re Amber
B.*, 1987 [California]; *State v. Rimmasch*, 1989 [Utah]). To determine
the law in their own states, professionals should consult attorneys
who are experts on child sexual abuse litigation.

Judges are more likely to allow testimony on whether abuse occurred when there is *no* jury. Jury trials usually occur in criminal
cases. Judges worry that jurors will put too much stock in the expert's
opinion. The jury, after all, must decide the case, not the expert. In
juvenile court, however, there is no jury, and concern that expert
testimony will overawe jurors is eliminated. The judge can keep the
expert's opinion in perspective. Thus, in juvenile court, a strong argument can be made that qualified professionals should be allowed to

offer an opinion on whether a child was sexually abused. The same argument can be made in custody litigation incident to divorce because in most states there is no jury in custody cases.

Before turning to expert testimony designed to rehabilitate a child's credibility, it is important to mention expert testimony that purports to identify the perpetrator of sexual abuse. Nothing in the professional literature suggests that experts on child sexual abuse possess special knowledge or expertise that allows them to identify the perpetrator of abuse. Expert witnesses should not offer an opinion that a particular person sexually abused a child.

EXPERT TESTIMONY TO REHABILITATE CHILDREN'S CREDIBILITY

One of the basic rules of our legal system is that the credibility of a witness cannot be supported or bolstered unless the witness's credibility is attacked. Thus, lawyers say, "You can't bolster your own witness." The process that attorneys use to attack the credibility of witnesses is called impeachment. The impeaching attorney attempts to persuade the jury that the witness should not be believed. (See Chapter 6 for discussion of impeachment.)

Suppose a prosecutor puts a child on the witness stand, and the child describes sexual abuse. The defense attorney does *not* attack the child's credibility. Since the child's credibility has not been impeached, the prosecutor cannot bolster the child's credibility. Suppose, however, as is often the case, the defense attorney *does* impeach the child's credibility in an effort to convince the jury to disbelieve the child. Once the child's credibility is attacked, judges sometimes allow expert testimony that is designed to rehabilitate the child's impaired credibility. Expert testimony designed to rehabilitate credibility is often called rebuttal testimony.

Expert Testimony on Delay in Reporting, Recantation, and Inconsistency

In child sexual abuse litigation, two forms of impeachment are particularly important. First, the defense attorney may assert that a child's behavior is inconsistent with allegations of abuse. For example, defense counsel may argue that a child should not be believed because the child did not report abuse for a substantial period of time, or because the child recanted. Such impeachment is legitimate. However, when the defense concentrates on delay, recantation, and certain other behaviors, the prosecutor may respond with expert testimony to inform jurors that such behavior is common in sexually abused children.

In the second form of impeachment, the defense attorney seeks to undermine the child's credibility by arguing that developmental differences between adults and children render children *as a group* less credible than adults. Defense counsel may assert that children are highly suggestible and have poor memories. In response to such impeachment, the prosecutor may offer expert testimony to inform jurors that children have adequate memories and are not as suggestible as many adults believe. (See Chapter 2 for discussion of children's memory and suggestibility.)

Delay in reporting child sexual abuse. Many victims of child sexual abuse never disclose their abuse (Russell, 1983). Of those who do disclose, delayed reporting is common (Finkelhor, 1979; Russell, 1986a, 1986b). Jones and McQuiston (1985) note that "people who have been sexually abused frequently delay reporting what has happened to them. All the major studies and case series consistently emphasize that delay is a major clinical feature of [child sexual abuse] cases" (p. 2). The reasons for delay are apparent. In intrafamilial abuse, the child is relatively helpless, and must accommodate to ongoing maltreatment (Summit, 1983). The abusing parent is often in a position to enforce secrecy. Many children are too embarrassed and ashamed to disclose their victimization.

Recantation. When disclosure occurs, many children refrain from telling the whole story, revealing a little at a time to "test the waters" and see how adults react (Sorensen & Snow, 1991). According to Jones and McQuiston (1985): "Usually children disclose a small portion of their total experience initially in an apparent attempt to test the adult's response before letting them know more about the assault. If they receive a positive and supportive response, they may feel safe enough to disclose more about their experience" (pp. 3-4). A young child who has been abused many times may begin by saying,

"He only did it once." Or "He never put it in me, he just touched me with it." Or "He only did it to the other kids, not to me." Such disclosure is inaccurate, of course, but considering the child's uncertainty, and the common belief among children that adults will think they are bad because they were abused, such behavior is understandable.

Victims disclose to friends, parents, teachers, school counselors, medical professionals, therapists, and others. Following disclosure, powerful forces may work to convince children to change the facts or recant. Such forces are particularly strong in intrafamilial abuse, where the perpetrator—with or without the cooperation of the non-abusing parent—pressures the child to change or deny allegations. There may be ample opportunity to instill fear, guilt, and ambivalence. As Jones and McQuiston (1985) state:

> After the disclosure has been made by the victims, the guilt connected with their participation in the abuse may intensify over the ensuing months. The feelings of guilt and personal responsibility may become combined with feelings of loss and grieving for the emotional warmth that the abuser provided. At that stage, it is difficult for the victim to appreciate that the warmth and emotional availability were only provided at a price. The victims begin to feel that they caused the family's break-up, and perhaps the incarceration of the abuser. Retraction may be a frequent accompaniment at this stage. (p. 7)

Summit (1983) describes the pressure to recant. Although this description does not apply to all cases, the picture Summit paints is accurate for many incest victims:

> Whatever a child says about sexual abuse, she is likely to reverse it. Beneath the anger of impulsive disclosure remains the ambivalence of guilt and the martyred obligation to preserve the family. In the chaotic aftermath of disclosure, the child discovers that the bedrock fears and threats underlying the secrecy are true. Her father abandons her and calls her a liar. . . . The family is fragmented, and all the children are placed in custody. The father is threatened with disgrace and imprisonment. The girl is blamed for causing the whole mess, and everyone seems to treat her like a freak. . . .
> The message from the mother is very clear, often explicit, "Why do you insist on telling those awful stories about your father? If you send

him to prison, we won't be a family anymore. We'll end up on welfare with no place to stay. Is that what you want to do to us?"

Once again, the child bears the responsibility of either preserving or destroying the family. The role reversal continues with the "bad" choice being to tell the truth and the "good" choice being to capitulate and restore a lie for the sake of the family.

Unless there is special support for the child and immediate intervention to force responsibility on the father, the girl will follow the "normal" course and retract her complaint. (p. 188; original emphasis removed)

Sorensen and Snow (1991) studied 116 cases of confirmed child sexual abuse: "In approximately 22% of the cases, children recanted their allegations. . . . Of those who recanted, 92% reaffirmed their abuse allegations over time" (p. 11).

Inconsistencies in children's descriptions of sexual abuse. Children who disclose sexual abuse are sometimes inconsistent in their descriptions of what happened. Inconsistency occurs for many reasons, three of which are particularly relevant to the present discussion.

First, when a child is repeatedly abused for months or years, individual molestations blur together (Hudson, 1990). If the child is asked to describe particular episodes, he or she may become confused, and confusion may lead to inconsistent versions of events.

Second, the psychological dynamics of disclosure lead many children to make inconsistent statements. Many children are ambivalent about their abusers, and mixed feelings cause some children to offer inconsistent accounts of abuse. In the study by Sorensen and Snow discussed above, the researchers write:

> Almost three-fourths of all the [116 sexually abused children] denied having been sexually abused. Denial statements were most commonly made (a) when children were initially questioned by a concerned parent or adult authority figure; and (b) when identified as potential victims and initially questioned in a formalized investigative process. Only 7% of the children who denied then moved directly to active disclosure. Tentative disclosure thus became the common middle step for the majority (78%) of these children. . . . approximately only one out of every ten children (11%) sampled were able to provide a disclosure of sexual abuse without denying or demonstrating tentative

features. . . . A strong majority (70%) gave further information over time about the sexually abusive activities.

. . .

Disclosure of child sexual abuse is best described by this research as a process, not an event. The common presumption that most abused children are capable of immediate active disclosure by providing a coherent, detailed account in an initial investigative interview is not supported by these findings, which suggest that only 11% of the subjects were in active disclosure at the time of the initial interview. (pp. 9-11)

The third reason for children's inconsistency relates to developmental immaturity (Fivush, Hamond, Harsch, Singer, & Wolf, 1991). The following discussion of children's inconsistency due to immaturity is drawn from the work of Karen N. Saywitz, Ph.D., of the Department of Psychiatry/UCLA/Harbor Medical Center, Los Angles.

Young children are particularly prone to inconsistency regarding peripheral details of events they have experienced. Young children have difficulty systematically evaluating their communications for possible errors, omissions, inconsistencies, or contradictions (Flavell, 1981; Singer & Flavell, 1981). An adult is capable of taking another person's perspective. Thus when one adult speaks to another, the speaker detects miscommunication by taking the listener's perspective. Unconsciously, the speaker thinks, Does the listener understand me? When the speaker detects miscommunication, it is a simple matter to stop and clarify. Young children have difficulty taking another person's perspective (Selman & Byrne, 1974), thus they have difficulty detecting miscommunication. Young children may not perceive the need to stop and clarify, with the result that a child's statement may contain inconsistencies an adult would detect and clarify.

Not only do young children have difficulty taking another person's perspective, they also have difficulty monitoring how well they understand messages *from* adults (Flavell, Speer, Green, & August, 1981; Ochs & Schieflin, 1979). This developmentally normal shortcoming can undermine children's performance. In one study, children were given instructions that omitted vital information. Nevertheless, 6-year-olds claimed to understand the instructions; 8-year-olds, on the other hand, were likely to ask for more information. The older children recognized that they did not understand (Markman,

1977, 1979). In another study, children were told that they could ask for clarifying information. Young children almost never requested more information, even when the information they were receiving was completely uninformative (Cosgrove & Patterson, 1977; Patterson, Massad, & Cosgrove, 1978).

These studies indicate that children have difficulty assessing what they do not know (Dickson, 1981). This lack of understanding limits children's ability to request clarification from adults, and may lead children to attempt to answer questions they do not comprehend. Unfortunately, young children rarely announce that they do not understand, and, as a consequence, children often seem less capable than they really are.

Children's understanding of cause and effect improves with age. Preschoolers occasionally baffle adults with extraordinary explanations of everyday events. In an oft-cited example, a preschooler insisted that a dog could make a train appear (Singer & Revenson, 1978). How did the dog accomplish this remarkable feat? By barking. The youngster thought the train appeared *because* the dog barked. The child did not understand what seems self-evident to adults: The dog barked because the train went by. The child was mistaken about the causal relationship between train and dog, but observe that the boy was correct about the basic facts. If the boy were being interviewed in a case where it was important to prove that a train went by or a dog barked, the child's mistaken—but developmentally understandable—reasoning about causation should not undermine his credibility. The youngster could describe the train and the dog.

Inconsistency can be caused by developmentally inappropriate questioning. Children are often asked questions about abstract concepts they do not comprehend, in language they do not understand. Children's responses can be misinterpreted as inconsistencies rather than misunderstandings. For example, suppose a young child is developmentally capable of understanding simple sentences 6 to 8 words long. The child is asked a complex question 30 words long, containing double negatives and embedded clauses. The youngster may respond to a part of the question that he or she understands, and ignore other parts that are crucial to adult understanding of the question and answer. Of course, the problem here is the question, not the child. Yet, adults may not realize that the question is developmentally inappropriate, and may erroneously conclude that the child is inconsistent.

Consider how often young children who have not learned to count are asked, How many times did it happen? A child may be capable of saying that something happened a lot or a little, or once or many times, but may be developmentally incapable of stating that it happened 5 times or 10. Unfortunately, because the child realizes that a response is expected, he or she may answer the question even without understanding it. The child may say something happened 5 times—not because that is how many times it happened, but because the child is familiar with the number 5, and feels compelled to say something. The answer may just as easily be 5,000. The child's misleading and irrelevant response was elicited because of the pressure to answer, and because young children do not understand that they can ask for clarification when they do not understand. Such lack of understanding results in inconsistent statements.

Ambivalence toward the abuser. In intrafamilial child sexual abuse, many victims are ambivalent about their abusers, feeling love and anger at the same time. It is not uncommon for an abused child to demonstrate affection toward the abusing parent, and to state a desire to live with the perpetrator.

Court decisions regarding expert testimony to rehabilitate children's credibility regarding delayed reporting, recantation, and related behaviors. In many child sexual abuse cases, the child is the state's most important witness. When the defense attorney tries to undermine the child's credibility, the question is whether the judge will allow expert testimony to rehabilitate the child's credibility.

Expert testimony on delayed reporting, recantation, inconsistency, and other matters. When children are impeached, judges in all states except Pennsylvania generally approve expert testimony that is designed to rehabilitate the children's credibility.[4] Expert testimony is admitted to explain why sexually abused children delay reporting abuse, why children recant, why children's descriptions of abuse are sometimes inconsistent, why abused children are angry, why some children want to live with the person who abused them, why a child abuse victim might appear "emotionally flat" following the assault, why a child might run away from home, and other behaviors (Myers, 1992). In *State v. Jensen* (1988), the defendant was charged with sexually abusing his 11-year-old stepdaughter. The child was acting out at school and demonstrating sexually inappropriate behavior. The defense attorney argued that the child fabricated the abuse "to deflect attention from her own misbehavior at school and to retaliate against the defendant's strict discipline" (p. 918). The Wisconsin Supreme Court approved expert testimony that the child's behavior at school was consistent with children who have been sexually abused. The expert's testimony provided an alternative explanation for the victim's behavior. The court wrote that "because a complainant's behavior frequently may not conform to commonly held expectations of how a victim reacts to sexual assault, courts admit expert opinion testimony to help juries avoid making decisions based on misconceptions of victim behavior" (p. 918).

Expert testimony on post-traumatic stress disorder and rape trauma syndrome, discussed previously, are sometimes allowed to rehabilitate victims' credibility.

Nonabusive parents sometimes delay reporting the abuse of their children. In *People v. McAlpin* (1991), the defendant was charged with molesting the daughter of the woman he was dating. The child's mother did not break off her relationship with the defendant immediately after learning of the molestation. Moreover, the mother had sexual intercourse with the defendant a week following the molestation. At trial, defense counsel sought to impeach the mother's "credibility by strongly implying that her behavior after the alleged incident was inconsistent with that of a mother who believed her daughter had been molested" (p. 570). The California Supreme Court approved expert "testimony that it is not unusual for a parent to refrain from reporting a known molestation of his or her child" (p. 569).

The following guidelines are suggested for professionals providing expert testimony to rehabilitate children's impeached credibility:

1. The prosecutor tells the judge and the defense attorney which behavior(s) the expert will discuss (*People v. Bowker*, 1988). For example, if the defense attorney limits the attack on the child's credibility to delay in reporting, the prosecutor lets the judge and defense counsel know

that the expert's testimony will be limited to helping the jury understand delay. The expert should limit testimony to the behavior emphasized by the defense attorney, and should not offer a wide-ranging lecture on children's reactions to sexual abuse.

2. In most cases, expert rehabilitation testimony is limited to a description of behaviors seen in sexually abused children *as a group*. It is often wise for the expert to avoid describing any particular child, and, in particular, to avoid describing the child in the present case.

3. If it is necessary to refer to the child in the present case, the expert should avoid using the word *victim*. Judges worry that referring to the child as a victim sends the jury a message that the expert knows the child was abused.

4. In most sexual abuse cases, expert witnesses should avoid reference to syndromes, such as child sexual abuse accommodation syndrome. It is not necessary to use the loaded word *syndrome* to help the jury understand that delay in reporting, recantation, and inconsistency are common in sexually abused children.

Expert testimony regarding developmental differences between children and adults. When the defense attorney seeks to undermine a child's credibility by asserting that developmental differences between children and adults render children *as a group* less credible than adults, it is sometimes appropriate to allow expert testimony. For example, the defense may attempt to convince the jury that young children are so suggestible that their testimony should be regarded with suspicion. The defense may point out that the child was interviewed numerous times, and that there was ample opportunity to plant the idea of abuse in the child's malleable young mind. Jurors may accept the argument that young children are dangerously suggestible. Faced with such impeachment, the state has a legitimate need to rehabilitate the child. The average juror is unaware of psychological research indicating that young children are not always more suggestible than older children and adults.

The defense attorney may argue that young children cannot differentiate fact from fantasy, and that the child lives in a fantasy world. Defense counsel might leave the jury with the impression that they cannot believe the testimony of a child who has an imaginary friend named Julius the Rabbit who talks to the child. Fantasy plays an important part in children's lives, but children can distinguish real from pretend (see Chapter 2). If defense counsel paints an inaccurate picture of a child's ability, expert rebuttal testimony is warranted.

There are not very many cases discussing expert testimony on developmental differences between children and adults. However, such expert testimony has been approved in several cases, and is entirely appropriate (*United States v. Azure*, 1986; see also Myers, 1992).

EXPERT TESTIMONY THAT
A PARTICULAR CHILD IS TRUTHFUL, OR THAT
SEXUALLY ABUSED CHILDREN AS A GROUP
GENERALLY TELL THE TRUTH ABOUT SEXUAL ABUSE

In child sexual abuse litigation, expert testimony on delay, recantation, and inconsistency has the *indirect* effect of bolstering the child's credibility. But are experts allowed to venture beyond indirect bolstering of credibility, and to offer a *direct* opinion that a particular child is telling the truth, or that sexually abused children as a group usually tell the truth about abuse? The answer from the courts is a resounding *no*. Virtually all American courts reject expert testimony that comments directly on the credibility of individual children or on the credibility of sexually abused children as a group. The Oregon Supreme Court did not mince words in its condemnation of expert testimony on the truthfulness of children. The court wrote: "We have said before, and we will say it again, but this time with emphasis—we really mean it—*no psychotherapist may render an opinion on whether a witness is credible in any trial conducted in this state.* The assessment of credibility is for the trier of fact and not for psychotherapists" (*State v. Milbradt*, 1988, p. 624). Courts reject expert testimony on credibility because judges firmly believe that assessment of credibility must be the exclusive province of the jury. As one court put it, "The jury is the lie detector in the courtroom" (*United States v. Barnard*, 1973, p. 912).

The fact that the law does not allow expert testimony on truthfulness does not mean professionals are devoid of knowledge on the subject. The literature contains information that is useful in detecting deliberately fabricated allegations of abuse (Myers et al., 1989). Outside the courtroom, professionals are free to continue their reliance on techniques that help differentiate true from false allegations of abuse. When it comes to courtroom testimony, however, experts should not state their belief that a child's description of abuse is truthful. Equally forbidden is an opinion that abused children as a group are truthful. For example, courts disapprove expert testimony that a certain percentage of sexually abused children are truthful (*State v. Moran*, 1986). The Arizona Supreme Court stated that professionals are not to offer "expert testimony that quantifies the probabilities of the credibility of another witness" (*State v. Lindsey*, 1986, p. 475).

EXPERT TESTIMONY
REGARDING THE ALLEGED PERPETRATOR

In the effort to prove that a person sexually abused a child, is the prosecutor allowed to offer expert testimony that the person fits the psychological profile of a sex offender or pedophile? For psychological as well as legal reasons, the answer should be no. The prosecutor should not offer such testimony, and mental health professionals should not provide it.

From the psychological perspective, the clinical and scientific literature indicates that persons who sexually abuse children are a heterogeneous group with few shared characteristics apart from a predilection for deviant sexual behavior with children. Furthermore, no psychological test or device reliably detects persons who have sexually abused children or are likely to do so. Thus, under the current state of scientific knowledge, there is no profile of a "typical" child molester (Myers et al., 1989, p. 142). Since there is no profile of a typical sex offender, there is no basis for expert testimony describing a profile.

From the legal perspective, the inappropriateness of profile testimony is clear when the reader understands one of the basic rules of American law. A prosecutor is not allowed to establish a person's guilt through evidence that the person has a particular character trait or propensity. For example, suppose Bill is accused of robbing the First National Bank. The prosecutor is not allowed to prove Bill's guilt with evidence that Bill robbed other banks in the past, and that, because of his propensity for bank robbery, Bill probably robbed First National Bank. Evidence of a person's character is not allowed to prove that the person acted in conformity with character on a particular occasion (Federal Rules of Evidence 404(a)). Put another way, the prosecutor cannot prove that Bill is guilty because "he is the *type* of guy who sticks up banks."

The rule against character evidence is applicable in sexual abuse litigation.[5] The prosecutor cannot establish guilt through expert testimony that the accused person has a character trait or propensity for sexual abuse. Expert testimony that the accused person fits the profile of a "typical" sex offender is essentially character evidence, and inadmissible for that reason. In *United States v. Gillespie* (1988), for example, the defendant was charged with sexual abuse of his 3-year-old goddaughter. The defendant acknowledged that the child had been abused, but he denied responsibility. The prosecutor offered "expert" testimony "that the characteristics of a molester include an early disruption in the family environment, often with one parent missing; a relationship with the parent of the opposite sex who is dominant; unsuccessful relationships with women; a poor self-concept; and general instability in the background" (p. 480). The court of appeals ruled that such testimony was improper evidence of defendant's character.

May the prosecutor offer expert testimony that there is *no* profile of a "typical" child molester or pedophile? In *People v. McAlpin* (1991), the California Supreme Court said yes. Such expert testimony helps the jury understand that child molesters come from all walks of life and backgrounds.

Unlike the prosecutor, the defendant in a criminal case *is* allowed to offer character evidence to prove innocence (Federal Rules of Evidence 404(a)(1)). Thus, in our bank robbery case, Bill could offer evidence that he is an honest, nonviolent person—not "the *type* of guy who sticks up banks." With this rule in mind, should a person accused of child sexual abuse be allowed to offer expert testimony that he or she does not fit the profile or share the character traits of child molesters? From the scientific perspective the answer should be no (*State v. Person*, 1989). The literature does not support the conclusion that there is a profile of a "typical" sex offender. Despite the lack of a reliable profile, some mental health professionals are willing to describe profiles, or to testify that a person does not share the characteristics of individuals who typically abuse children, and a few courts allow such testimony (*People v. Stoll*, 1989).

Once the defendant offers expert testimony that he or she does not share the characteristics of child molesters, the prosecutor is allowed to offer expert testimony to contradict the defendant's expert witness.

❏ Expert Testimony in Neglect Litigation

When children suffer serious physical or sexual abuse, the need for intervention is clear. Intervention to prevent neglect, however, is sometimes not as clear-cut. Neglect is a protean concept that involves an infinite variety of situations that rob children of care, protection, and development. Professionals from medicine, psychology, and social work play a valuable role in helping judges decide when judicial intervention is warranted. This section briefly describes eight categories of neglect.

MEDICAL NEGLECT

Parents have a legal as well as a moral duty to provide necessary medical care for their children. When parents fail or refuse to provide such care, the juvenile court may authorize care over parental objection. Parental failure to provide essential medical care is called medical neglect.

Parents who refuse medical care for their children often do so on the basis of religious belief. Parents argue that state-enforced medical care violates the parents' constitutional right to freedom of religion. When parental religious belief stands as a barrier to essential medical care for children, however, judges often intervene. As the Arizona Supreme Court put it, "If there is a direct collision of a child's right to good health and a parent's religious beliefs, the parent's rights must give way" (*Matter of Appeal in Cochise County Juvenile Action*, 1982, p. 465).

The willingness of judges to override religious objections to medical care for children is based on the distinction between freedom to believe in a particular religion and freedom to act on religious belief. As long ago as 1878, the U.S. Supreme Court stated that religious belief is completely beyond government control, but action "in violation of social duties" may be prohibited (*Reynolds v. United States*, 1878, p. 164). The Supreme Court reiterated this position in 1972, when it wrote that "the power of the parent, even when linked to a free exercise [of religion] claim, may be subject to limitation . . . if it appears that parental decisions will jeopardize the health and safety of the child" (*Wisconsin v. Yoder*, 1972, pp. 233-234).

In medical neglect cases, it is useful to distinguish between cases in which treatment is needed to save a child's life and those in which treatment is important, but not essential to preserve life.

Medical Treatment
Needed to Save a Child's Life

Many judges have ordered life-saving medical care over parental objection. The Massachusetts Supreme Judicial Court observed that "courts which have considered the question . . . uniformly have decided that State intervention is appropriate where the medical treatment sought is necessary to save the child's life" (*Custody of a Minor*, 1978, p. 1062). When a child's life hangs in the balance, and the proposed treatment is likely to cure or substantially improve the child's condition, judges usually intervene.

> *When a child's life hangs in the balance, judges usually intervene.*

Treatment Not Essential
to Save a Child's Life

When parents refuse consent to medical care that is important for their child's well-being but that is not essential to preserve life, judges reach different results, sometimes deferring to parental authority, sometimes not. Cases turn on their unique facts. It is important to note, however, that all states permit some intervention in non-life-threatening situations.

In non-life-threatening cases, judges rely on several principles in deciding whether or not to override parental objections to medical care. The most important factor is the harm a child will suffer without court-ordered medical care. The greater the harm, the more likely the judge will intervene. When harm approaches an imminent threat to the child's life, the judge relies on court decisions that permit intervention in life-and-death cases.

The judge considers the kind of medical problem involved and whether the problem is progressive or stable. The judge considers the treatment required to alleviate the problem and whether the treatment is well accepted and reliable or experimental. The judge evaluates the likelihood of successful treatment, and the risks and side effects of treatment. Generally speaking, as side effects and risk of treatment increase, judges demonstrate correspondingly greater deference to parental decision making. The same is true as the likelihood of successful treatment decreases. The less likely treatment is to succeed, the more likely the judge is to deny intervention and defer to parental authority. Even when successful treatment is likely, a judge may defer to parents when the treatment entails painful or unpleasant side effects for the child. The judge considers the likelihood that treatment will provide the child a normal and meaningful life, or as normal and meaningful a life as is possible considering the child's condition.

When the child is old enough to express a preference, the judge considers the child's wishes. With mature adolescents, the judge may defer to the adolescent's wishes. In a thoughtful decision, the Illinois Supreme Court discussed the propriety of allowing mature adolescents to make most treatment decisions for themselves, even in life-and-death situations (*In re E.G.*, 1990). The adolescent in the Illinois case, whose initials were E.G., was 17 years old. E.G. had leukemia and needed blood transfusions, but E.G. and her mother refused the transfusions because they were Jehovah's Witnesses. The state filed a dependency petition in juvenile court. The evidence presented to the judge showed that even with transfusions, the likelihood that E.G. would survive was only 20-25%. E.G. testified that "the decision to refuse blood transfusions was her own and that she fully understood the nature of her disease and the consequences of her decision." Expert testimony from a psychiatrist disclosed that E.G. had the maturity of an 18- to 21-year-old adult. E.G.'s decision was respected, and on appeal, the Illinois Supreme Court offered the following guidelines:

> The paramount issue raised by this appeal is whether a minor like E.G. has a right to refuse medical treatment. In Illinois, an adult has a common law right to refuse medical treatment, even if it is of a life-sustaining nature. . . . This court has also held that an adult may refuse life-saving blood transfusions on first amendment free exercise of religion grounds. . . . An infant child, however, can be compelled to accept life-saving medical treatment over the objections of her parents. . . . In the matter before us, E.G. was a minor, but one who was just months shy of her eighteenth birthday, and an individual that the record indicates was mature for her age. Although the age of majority in Illinois is 18, that age is not an impenetrable barrier that magically precludes a minor from possessing and exercising certain rights normally associated with adulthood. Numerous exceptions are found in this jurisdiction and others which treat minors as adults under specific circumstances. . . .
>
> The trial judge must determine whether a minor is mature enough to make health care choices on her own. . . . We feel the intervention of a judge is appropriate for two reasons. First, Illinois public policy values the sanctity of life. . . . When a minor's health and life are at stake, this policy becomes a critical consideration. A minor may have a long and fruitful life ahead that an immature, foolish decision could jeopardize. Consequently, when the trial judge weighs the evidence in making a determination of whether a minor is mature enough to handle a health care decision, he must find proof of this maturity by clear and convincing evidence. Second, the State has a *parens patriae* power to protect those incompetent to protect themselves. . . . "It is well-settled that the State as *parens patriae* has a special duty to protect minors and, if necessary, make vital decisions as to whether to submit a minor to necessary treatment where the condition is life threatening, as wrenching and distasteful as such actions may be." . . . The State's *parens patriae* power pertaining to minors is strongest when the minor is immature and thus incompetent (lacking in capacity) to make these decisions on her own. The *parens patriae* authority fades, however, as the minor gets older and disappears upon her reaching adulthood. The State interest in protecting a mature minor in these situations will vary depending upon the nature of the medical treatment involved. Where the

health care issues are potentially life threatening, the State's *parens patriae* interest is greater than if the health care matter is less consequential.

Therefore, the trial judge must weigh these two principles against the evidence he receives of a minor's maturity. If the evidence is clear and convincing that the minor is mature enough to appreciate the consequences of her actions, and that the minor is mature enough to exercise the judgment of an adult, then the mature minor doctrine affords her the common law right to consent to or refuse medical treatment. . . . However, this common law right is not absolute. The right must be balanced against four State interests: (1) the preservation of life; (2) protecting the interests of third parties; (3) prevention of suicide; and (4) maintaining the ethical integrity of the medical profession. . . . Of these four concerns, protecting the interests of third parties is clearly the most significant here. The principal third parties in these cases would be parents, guardians, adult siblings, and other relatives. If a parent or guardian opposes an unemancipated mature minor's refusal to consent to treatment for a life-threatening health problem, this opposition would weigh heavily against the minor's right to refuse. In this case, for example, had E.G. refused the transfusions *against* the wishes of her mother, then the court would have given serious consideration to her mother's desires. (pp. 325-328)

FAILURE TO THRIVE

Failure to thrive can be caused by medical problems or extreme neglect (Schmitt & Mauro, 1989). It is always important to rule out medical explanations for failure to thrive. The term *nonorganic failure to thrive* describes failure to thrive that is attributable to neglect. The DSM-III-R uses the phrase "reactive attachment disorder of infancy or early childhood" to describe the psychological damage caused by extreme emotional neglect (American Psychiatric Association, 1987).

One way to confirm a diagnosis of nonorganic failure to thrive or reactive attachment disorder is to remove the child from the home and see if the child improves. In a Massachusetts case, the child had reactive attachment disorder. While in parental custody, the child was depressed, tense, and unresponsive to people or toys, except toys shaped like food. In court, the mother's attorney objected to evidence that the child's condition improved significantly when the child was removed from the mother's custody. The Massachusetts

Supreme Judicial Court wrote that "it was not error for the judge to consider evidence of the child's condition . . . while he lived with the mother, and contrast it with the development of the child since he had been removed from the mother's custody" (*Petition of Catholic Charitable Bureau of Archdiocese of Boston*, 1985, p. 153; see also *Reuben & Elizabeth O. v. Department of Human Services*, 1986).

PSYCHOLOGICAL NEGLECT

No aspect of neglect is more difficult to define than psychological neglect (Cicchetti & Nurcombe, 1991; Hart & Brassard, 1991). A useful approach to psychological maltreatment is contained in Garbarino, Guttmann, and Seeley's book *The Psychologically Battered Child* (1986). The authors describe five parental behaviors that constitute psychological maltreatment:

1. *Rejecting:* The adult refuses to acknowledge the child's worth and the legitimacy of the child's needs.
2. *Isolating:* The adult cuts the child off from normal social experiences, prevents the child from forming friendships, and makes the child believe that he or she is alone in the world.
3. *Terrorizing:* The adult verbally assaults the child, creates a climate of fear, bullies and frightens the child, and makes the child believe that the world is capricious and hostile.
4. *Ignoring:* The adult deprives the child of essential stimulation and responsiveness, stifling emotional growth and intellectual development.
5. *Corrupting:* The adult "mis-socializes" the child, stimulates the child to engage in destructive antisocial behavior, reinforces that deviance, and makes the child unfit for normal experience. (p. 8)

Garbarino and his colleagues do not describe when these parental behaviors justify legal intervention. Nevertheless, their categories provide a useful starting place for analysis. Clearly, juvenile court intervention is justified in some cases. The Colorado Supreme Court said it well: "The welfare of the child cannot be protected if courts must ignore the very real emotional abuses that a child may suffer. Emotional abuse may leave scars more permanent and damaging to a child's personality than bodily bruises from a physical beating" (*People v. D.A.K.*, 1979, p. 750). Indeed, the consensus of professional opinion appears to be that psychological neglect is the core issue of all child maltreatment (Hart, Germain, & Brassard, 1987; see also Briere & Runtz, 1990; Claussen & Crittenden, 1991; Vissing, Straus, Gelles, & Harrop, 1991).

Juvenile court intervention is warranted when a child is suffering serious psychological disturbance caused by deliberate psychological abuse. Intervention may also be appropriate when parents who did not cause their child's psychological suffering refuse to obtain professional services for the child.

Difficult questions arise when a child is on the verge of psychological damage, but has not developed serious symptoms. The following guidelines are offered to help professionals decide when juvenile court intervention may be appropriate to *prevent* psychological harm:

1. There must be an *imminent* risk that the child will suffer specific, serious, short- or long-term psychological harm caused by deliberate psychological abuse. The risk of serious harm can be equally imminent when parents who do not cause the child's condition refuse to get help.
2. Parents must refuse to alter their behavior, or the judge must be persuaded the parents cannot or will not alter their behavior.
3. The likelihood of harm must be based on more than speculation. There must be persuasive, documented evidence that serious harm is very likely.

Under these guidelines, intervention is sometimes appropriate to *prevent* psychological damage. Garbarino et al. advise, however, that even though the risk to a child is high, it may be appropriate to forgo legal intervention when the child has an ongoing, nurturing relationship with an adult. Such a relationship may buffer the child from the damage caused by psychologically neglectful parents. Garbarino et al. provide detailed information on psychological evaluation of parents and children.

MENTALLY RETARDED PARENTS

Judges agree that parental mental retardation is not a sufficient reason to intervene in the family. There must be evidence that mental retardation impairs the parent's ability to provide minimally adequate child care. The scientific literature increasingly disputes the idea that mentally retarded persons as a group are incapable of adequate parenting. Tymchuk and Andron (1990) write that "although it is clear that the provision of adequate child care requires a certain intellectual level, it is unclear what that level is" (p. 313). Some parents with IQs below 70 provide adequate care. Clearly, cases involving mentally retarded parents must be decided on a case-by-case basis, and it is inappropriate to presume parental incompetence. It is equally inappropriate to presume that most mentally retarded parents are incapable of benefiting from parenting training. However, when a parent's mental retardation causes harm or the risk of harm to a child, intervention is proper.

The Indiana Court of Appeal reflected the dominant judicial viewpoint in a case involving termination of the parental rights of two mentally retarded parents (*Matter of Dull*, 1988). The parents' IQs were 62 and 72. Their two children were developmentally delayed, and one was psychologically disturbed. The developmental delay and psychological disturbance resulted from inadequate parenting. The parents dutifully attended court-ordered counseling classes, but because of their intellectual limitations, they were unable to benefit from the classes. The Indiana Court of Appeal affirmed the trial judge's decision terminating the parent-child relationship. The appellate court wrote that it is proper to consider a parent's "mental retardation as a factor in deciding whether or not to terminate . . . parental rights" (p. 976). The court wrote that "retardation of a parent by itself is not a ground for termination of parental rights" (p. 976). The court noted, however, that "the majority of jurisdictions recognize that while an adjudication of a parent's mental retardation will not alone render that parent unfit, 'evidence of such adjudication may be considered, along with all other pertinent evidence bearing upon the question of that parent's fitness' " (p. 976).

The fact that a mentally retarded parent has a child who is handicapped and has special needs may be considered by the judge in deciding whether the parent can provide adequate care (*Adoption of Abigail*, 1986).

PSYCHIATRICALLY DISABLED PARENTS

As is true with mental retardation, parental mental illness alone is not a sufficient basis to intervene in the family. When mental illness impairs ability to provide for a child's needs, however, intervention is sometimes appropriate. Expert testimony that gives specific examples of how a parent's mental illness is likely to harm a child is useful (*In re Jamie M.*, 1982).

ABANDONMENT

Abandonment is often used as a ground for termination of parental rights; it is equally viable as a basis for initial intervention. Abandonment is usually defined as parental conduct indicating a willful disregard of the obligations of parenthood. Abandonment may be established through objective evidence of the parent's conduct, or through evidence of the parent's actual subjective intent to abandon a child (*D.M. v. State*, 1973).

Up to a point, abandonment is reversible (*Black v. Gray*, 1988). A parent who abandons a child may attempt to reestablish the parent-child relationship. However, abandonment is not washed away by minimal efforts to reestablish a relationship (*In re Adoption of T.M.*, 1989), and parents have only so long to act. If a parent's attempts to communicate with a child are thwarted by others, the parent has not abandoned the child (*Sharon H. v. Foster*, 1989).

SUBSTANCE ABUSE AS NEGLECT

The literature reveals that parental substance abuse is highly correlated with child neglect and abuse (Bays, 1990; Famularo, Stone, Barnum, & Wharton, 1986). Professionals who work with substance-abusing parents know that many such parents do not comply with court-ordered treatment plans. Famularo, Kinscherff, Burnshaft, Spivak, and Fenton (1989) studied juvenile court cases involving substance-abusing parents and concluded that professionals cannot rely on a court order to ensure cooperation from parents. Murphy et al. (1991) found a high frequency of parental substance abuse in a sample of juvenile court cases involving serious child maltreatment. Some parents condone or actually encourage the use of alcohol and other drugs by their school-age and adolescent children. Such behavior constitutes psychological neglect.

Properly qualified experts can help the juvenile court judge understand that unless parental substance abuse is controlled, there is little hope that abuse or neglect of children will stop.

GENERAL NEGLECT

Some of the most difficult neglect cases involve children living in disorganized and often filthy homes, where their physical and psychological needs are not met, but where it is difficult to find a clear "handle" on which to justify intervention. Judges are hesitant to intervene in families where poverty is the reason a child's needs are not met. As the Massachusetts Supreme Judicial Court wrote, "A parent may not be found unfit because he or she is poor" (*Petition of Catholic Charitable Bureau*, 1985, p. 148). Yet some poor children are genuinely neglected and in need of protection. It is often difficult to determine when a child's problems are caused by poverty and when by maltreatment.

Intervention is warranted when a child's physical or psychological well-being is significantly harmed, or when the risk of such harm is high, and when the totality of the circumstances indicates that neglect has occurred. As the Utah Supreme Court remarked, "Children are entitled to the care of an adult who cares enough to provide the child with the opportunity to form psychological bonds, in addition to the physical necessities of life. . . . An unfit or incompetent parent is one who substantially and repeatedly refuses or fails to render proper parental care and protection" (*In re K.S.*, 1987, pp. 172-173). Most parents provide the love and affection their children need to grow physically and mentally. When the evidence indicates that a parent does not care enough to provide for a child's basic needs, however, intervention is appropriate.

❏ **Special Issues in Child Abuse and
Neglect Litigation in Juvenile Court**

This final section describes three issues that arise in juvenile court: sibling petitions, intervention justified by a parent's failure to protect a child, and reasonable efforts to keep families together.

SIBLING PETITIONS

Suppose one child has been abused or neglected, but another child in the same family has not been harmed. CPS files a petition in juvenile court to protect *both* children. As evidence of danger to the unharmed child, CPS points to the abuse of the sibling. May the judge protect the unharmed child on the basis of harm to the sibling? Judicial decisions make clear that in some cases a parent's abuse or neglect of one child can be used to prove that another child is endangered (*Matter of Schmeltzer*, 1989; *Matter of T.C.*, 1989). The law does not require CPS to wait until a child is injured.

INTERVENTION JUSTIFIED BY
PARENT'S FAILURE TO PROTECT A CHILD

In some cases, a parent's failure to protect a child from abuse or neglect inflicted by another adult justifies intervention. The Arizona Court of Appeals stated that a finding of neglect may be based on one parent's failure to prevent abuse by another parent (*Matter of Appeal in Pima County Juvenile Dependency Action No. 96290*, 1990). The court went on to state that one parent's refusal to acknowledge abuse perpetrated by the other may justify intervention.

REASONABLE EFFORTS

In 1980, Congress enacted the Adoption Assistance and Child Welfare Act, commonly referred to as Public Law 96-272. A key provision of the act requires that "reasonable efforts" be made to prevent removal of neglected and abused children from their homes, and to reunify families when children have been removed. The reasonable efforts requirement of the federal law is designed to ensure that families are provided necessary services. The act requires the juvenile court judge to scrutinize the social welfare agency's efforts in every case to determine whether reasonable efforts were made. A judicial finding of reasonable efforts is necessary at all crucial stages, including shelter care, disposition, and review hearings.

Interestingly, Congress did not define *reasonable efforts*. It is up to individual states to give meaning to the term. At a minimum, reasonable efforts include (a) identifying the exact danger that puts the child at risk of placement and that justifies intervention, (b) determining how family problems are causing or contributing to the danger, and (c) providing services to alleviate or diminish the danger to the child. Efforts are reasonable when they are *real* and not imaginary or found only on paper, when they are individually tailored to the specific problems that require intervention, and when they are sufficient in intensity and duration to provide an opportunity for change.

What if a judge finds that the agency has not made reasonable efforts to prevent removal of a child or to reunify a family? Does lack of reasonable efforts mean the judge cannot remove a child from a dangerous environment? Does lack of reasonable efforts following removal mean the judge must put the child back into a dangerous environment? The answer, on both counts, is no. The law does not link the judge's ability to remove children from their parents to the reasonable efforts requirement. The child's safety is always paramount. The only ramification if the judge finds that the agency failed to make reasonable efforts is that the agency may not be able to claim federal matching funds for the child's stay in foster care.

Parents must make efforts too. As the Utah Court of Appeals put it, "Rehabilitation is a two-way street which requires commitment on the part of the parents, as well as the availability of services from the State" (*In re P.H.*, 1989, p. 572).

❏ Notes

1. In some criminal cases there is no jury, and the judge fulfills the fact-finding responsibility normally entrusted to a jury. In juvenile and family court, there usually is no jury. When there is no jury, the judge permits expert testimony if the testimony will assist the judge. In this chapter, the word *jury* is used to describe the fact finder, whether the fact finder is a jury or the judge.

2. Depending on the discipline of the expert witness, this question changes slightly. Common variations include "reasonable scientific certainty," "reasonable medical certainty," and "reasonable clinical certainty."

3. Consent is not a defense to a charge of child sexual abuse. Nevertheless, consent sometimes plays a subsidiary role in child sexual abuse litigation.

4. Pennsylvania appears to be the only state that does not allow at least some expert testimony to rehabilitate children's impeached credibility (*Commonwealth v. Dunkle*, 1992).

5. Quite a few states do allow a type of character evidence in child sexual abuse litigation. These states allow the prosecutor to prove that the accused person has committed sexual offenses for which the accused person is not now on trial. The use of the accused person's other sexual offenses is a type of character evidence. Nevertheless, states allowing such evidence create an exception to the general rule that a person's guilt cannot be established with evidence of the person's character (see Myers, 1992).

6

Cross-Examination and Impeachment

Two types of witnesses testify in court: lay witnesses and expert witnesses. A lay witness is an individual with personal knowledge of relevant facts. The lay witness relates those facts to the jury. An example of a lay witness is an eyewitness to a crime. An expert witness is a person with special knowledge, experience, or education, who helps the jury understand technical, clinical, or scientific issues. An example of an expert witness is a mental health professional who explains the dynamics of child sexual abuse. (See Chapter 5 for discussion of expert testimony.)

In child abuse and neglect litigation, professionals provide both lay and expert testimony. To illustrate, suppose a child discloses sexual abuse to a teacher. The child is interviewed by a social worker and examined by a nurse practitioner. The child's disclosure is a relevant fact, and the teacher has personal knowledge of the disclosure. The teacher testifies as a lay witness, and repeats the child's disclosure. The social worker also testifies as a lay witness by repeating what the child said during the interview. The nurse practitioner provides a combination of lay and expert testimony. He or she testifies as a lay witness when repeating what the child said, and testifies as an expert witness when providing an opinion about the results of the physical examination of the child.

Testifying begins with direct examination. During direct examination, the witness answers questions from the attorney who asked the witness to testify. The purpose of direct examination is usually to elicit information favorable to the party on whose behalf the witness testifies. Following direct examination, the opposing attorney has the right to cross-examine. Cross-examination is sometimes followed by redirect examination. Redirect examination affords the attorney who asked the witness to testify an opportunity to clarify issues that were discussed during cross-examination. Finally, in rare cases, redirect examination is followed by re-cross-examination.

Attorneys view cross-examination as essential to the search for truth. A leading legal commentator has written, "For two centuries, common law judges and lawyers have regarded the opportunity of cross-examination as an essential safeguard of the accuracy and completeness of testimony, and they have insisted that the opportunity is a right and not a mere privilege" (McCormick, 1984, p. 47). Another leading commentator states that cross-examination "is beyond any doubt the greatest legal engine ever invented for the discovery of truth" (Wigmore, 1974, § 1367).

Cross-examination causes anxiety. It is disturbing because it is adversarial and a bit mysterious. Nonlawyers generally are not privy to the secrets of the cross-examiner's art. The following discussion is intended to demystify cross-examination by explaining the techniques and strategies of the cross-examiner. Understanding the art of cross-examination—going behind enemy lines, if you will —reduces anxiety and allows professionals to deal on more equal terms with the cross-examiner.

Basically, there are two types of cross-examination: positive and negative. The purposes of negative cross-examination are to attack the witness's credibility or impartiality and to undermine the witness's testimony. Negative cross-examination is risky. When a witness is attacked, he or she resists providing information favorable to the attacker. Furthermore, the witness is prone to find opportunities to refute points the cross-examiner is trying to make. Positive cross-examination avoids many of these risks. With positive cross-examination, the attorney avoids attacking the witness and uses a positive, even friendly, approach in the hope of eliciting information favorable to his or her client. For example, the attorney might limit cross-examination to reiterating parts of the witness's direct testimony that can be viewed as favorable to the cross-examiner's client.

When an attorney uses negative cross-examination, he or she hopes to impeach the witness's credibility. Impeachment is the primary goal of negative cross-examination. No two cross-examiners are alike, of course, and each attorney's style is influenced by his or her own personality and experience. Nevertheless, attorneys usually select from several impeachment techniques. The techniques described in the next section are used primarily with lay witnesses, although some are also used with expert witnesses. Impeachment techniques reserved primarily for expert witnesses are discussed later in this chapter.

❑ Impeachment of Lay Witnesses

This section briefly describes six impeachment techniques available to the cross-examiner.

IMPEACHMENT WITH THE WITNESS'S PRIOR STATEMENTS THAT ARE INCONSISTENT WITH THE WITNESS'S TESTIMONY IN COURT

A witness's testimony may be impeached with evidence that prior to testifying, the witness told a different story. "The theory of attack by prior inconsistent statements is not based on the assumption that the present testimony is false and the former statement true but rather upon the notion that talking one way on the stand and another way previously is blowing hot and cold, and raises a doubt as to the truthfulness of both statements" (McCormick, 1984, p. 74).

When the cross-examiner confronts a witness with a prior inconsistent statement, the witness is usually allowed to explain the inconsistency.

BIAS

Testimony from biased witnesses is subject to doubt, and the cross-examiner is allowed to ask questions designed to bring out bias or favoritism. McCormick (1984) notes that the law "recognizes the slanting effect upon human testimony of the emotions or feelings of the witness toward the parties or the self-interest of the witness in the outcome of the case. . . . Partiality, or any acts, relationships or motives reasonably likely to produce it, may be proved to impeach credibility" (p. 85).

EVIDENCE THAT THE WITNESS HAS A CHARACTER TRAIT FOR UNTRUTHFULNESS

A witness may be impeached with evidence that the witness is an untruthful person. The theory of such impeachment is that an untruthful person may be willing to lie under oath. The cross-examiner is allowed to confront the witness with specific instances of the witness's behavior that tend to prove untruthfulness.

CONVICTION OF CERTAIN CRIMES

It is human nature to question the testimony of people who have been convicted of serious crimes, particularly crimes involving deceit or fraud. Within limits that vary from state to state, the cross-examining attorney is permitted to impeach a witness by proving that the witness was convicted of a crime.

DEFECTS IN CAPACITY

A witness may be impeached with evidence that his or her ability to perceive, remember, or communicate is impaired.

INADEQUATE OPPORTUNITY TO OBSERVE EVENTS

A common method of impeachment is to prove that the witness did not have a good opportunity to observe an event. For example, if a witness testifies that a car was weaving as it sped down the road, the cross-examiner may bring out the fact that it was dark at the time, and that the witness had only a brief glimpse of the car.

❑ Impeachment of Expert Witnesses

When cross-examining an expert witness, the attorney may use the impeachment techniques described above. In addition, attorneys draw on the following principles to impeach expert witnesses: (a) In most cases, cross-examiners avoid a frontal attack; (b) in appropriate cases, they conduct only positive cross-examination, avoiding, or at least postponing, negative cross-examination; (c) they attempt to raise doubts about experts' testimony that can be used during their closing arguments to the jury; and (d) they raise the possibility of bias.

AVOIDING A FRONTAL ATTACK

When people think of cross-examination, they think of Perry Mason or an attorney on *L.A. Law*, ruthlessly burrowing in on a perspiring witness until the beleaguered witness finally blurts out, "All right, you win, I did it." That may be the way it is on TV, but such dramatic cross-examination is seldom seen in real courtrooms, especially with expert witnesses. The skilled cross-examiner seldom attempts a frontal attack in the hope of utterly destroying the expert's credibility or getting the expert to change position. Why do cross-examiners avoid the frontal attack? Because it usually fails. Moreover, jurors may react negatively to a cross-examiner who ruthlessly attacks an expert, especially an expert in the business of helping children, and the jury's discontent with the attorney may generalize to the client. Thus skilled cross-examiners seldom use the sledgehammer, preferring instead more subtle techniques.

CONDUCTING A POSITIVE CROSS-EXAMINATION

As discussed earlier, cross-examination can be positive or negative. In appropriate cases, with some experts, the attorney avoids the risks of negative cross-examination and limits cross-examination to the positive approach. If the cross-examiner's questions are fair and accurate, the professional should agree with them. There is nothing wrong with agreeing with the cross-examiner. In fact, an expert witness who stubbornly refuses to give an inch in the face of reasonable questions undermines his or her own credibility in the eyes of the jury.

When the cross-examiner intends to conduct a negative cross-examination, he or she may begin with a positive approach, hoping to elicit favorable information before the witness is alerted—and alienated—by the onset of negative questions. Professionals who may be called as expert witnesses should remember that even if a cross-examiner uses a positive approach at the beginning, the negative segment of cross-examination may be just around the corner.

RAISING DOUBTS ABOUT THE EXPERT'S TESTIMONY

At the end of the case, the attorneys present closing arguments. One goal of closing argument is to persuade the jury that certain witnesses should not be believed. With this goal in mind, the attorney uses cross-examination to raise questions and doubts about the expert's testimony; during closing argument, the attorney will remind the jury of those questions and doubts.

Attorneys know that they are unlikely to hit the jackpot during cross-examination. The expert is not likely to do a complete about-face and change the opinion he or she gave during direct examination. Therefore, attorneys use indirect methods to undermine the testimony of experts. The cross-examiner abandons the idea of a direct hit, and hopes instead to poke a few little holes in the expert's testimony, to raise a few questions. These questions are *deliberately left unanswered* until the cross-examiner's closing argument to the jury, when the expert is safely off the witness stand and unable to explain or clarify as the cross-examiner painstakingly reminds the jury of the little holes in the expert's testimony and answers those unanswered questions. Needless to say, the cross-examiner's answers are quite different from those the expert would give. But the attorney, not the expert, has the last word with the jury.

How does the cross-examiner accomplish the goal of raising questions and doubts about the expert's testimony that can be used against the expert during the attorney's closing argument? The answer lies in the attorney's ability to control cross-examination. Control of witnesses is accomplished in three ways: (a) by asking leading questions, (b) by limiting the witness's opportunity to explain answers, and (c) by using a technique called "hiding the ball."

Leading Questions

The attorney conducting direct examination is generally not allowed to ask leading questions. By contrast, the cross-examiner *is* permitted to use leading questions, and some attorneys ask *only* leading questions during cross-examination. A leading question suggests the answer to the question. For example, suppose the cross-examiner wants the expert to acknowledge that a child recanted. The cross-examiner controls the witness by using leading questions that require short, specific answers—answers the attorney wants the jury to hear. The attorney might say, "It's true, isn't it, that Sally recanted her allegations?" Or, "The child recanted more than once, didn't she?" The questions permit only short, specific answers, preferably limited to yes or no.

The cross-examiner keeps the witness hemmed in with leading questions, and seldom asks why or how something happened. How and why questions permit the witness to explain, and explanation is precisely what the cross-examiner does not want. Naturally, when a question calls for a simple yes or no, it is often necessary to expand on the answer. With Sally's recantation, for example, the jury should know that she recanted because her life was threatened. But the cross-examiner tries to limit the witness's ability to explain, and this is where the second aspect of witness control comes in.

Limiting the Witness's Ability to Explain

When the witness tries to explain, the attorney may interrupt and say, "Please just answer yes or no." If the witness persists, the attorney may ask the judge to admonish the witness to limit answers to the questions asked. Expert witnesses are understandably frustrated when the cross-examiner thwarts their efforts to clarify their testimony. The expert may silently wonder, "How can this process possibly lead to the truth? The cross-examiner's questions paint a completely one-sided picture, and the attorney refuses to let me give balanced and complete answers to the questions?!" This frustration is understandable, but before giving up on the adversary system of justice, the expert should remember three things.

First, the cross-examiner has *one* overriding responsibility: to represent the client zealously. The cross-examiner's job is to present the client's view of the facts, not to permit the expert witness *another* opportunity to repeat unfavorable testimony.

> *The cross-examiner has one overriding responsibility: to represent the client zealously*

To represent the client's interests adequately, the cross-examiner must have fairly wide latitude to control the course of cross-examination, and to control what the expert—who is an adverse witness—is permitted to say.

Second, sometimes it is proper to say, "Counsel, it is not possible for me to answer with a simple yes or no. May I explain myself?" Chadwick (1990) advises, "When a question is posed in a strictly 'yes or no' fashion, but the correct answer is 'maybe,' the witness should find a way to express the true answer. A direct appeal to the judge may be helpful in some cases" (p. 967). Many judges permit witnesses to explain themselves during cross-examination if the jury needs more information to make sense of the witness's testimony.

Finally, remember that after cross-examination comes redirect examination, during which the attorney who asked the expert to testify is allowed to ask further questions. During redirect examination the expert has an opportunity to clarify matters that were left unclear during cross-examination.

Hiding the Ball

The third witness control technique, "hiding the ball," is used when the cross-examiner wants the expert witness to concede a point the expert will deny if the cross-examiner comes right out and asks. The cross-examiner conceals the real purpose of cross-examination, which is to lead the unsuspecting witness into a trap. By the time the witness figures out what the cross-examiner has in mind, it is too late, and the witness has to concede the cross-examiner's point.

How does the cross-examiner hide the ball? He or she asks a series of apparently innocuous questions that do not seem related to sensitive topics. In this way the witness does not perceive the need to answer carefully. The cross-examiner uses leading questions, so the expert has to answer as the examiner desires. But since the questions seem harmless, the witness goes along. To keep the witness off balance, and to keep the ultimate objective hidden, the cross-examiner bounces from topic to topic; always returning, however, to questions that lead to the ultimate objective. Gradually, through a series of carefully structured questions, the cross-examiner locks the witness into a predetermined position. Only then, when the witness is painted into a corner, does the cross-examiner raise the subject he or she had in mind all along.

With this subtle cat-and-mouse game in mind, it is easy to see why it is important for expert witnesses to keep their guard up. The skilled cross-examiner is like a good chess player, always thinking two or three moves ahead. This is not to say, however, that the expert witness should try to out lawyer the lawyer, or guess where the lawyer is going with questions. Experts get in trouble when they stop concentrating on the questions and try to play the lawyer's game. The best course for the witness is simply to listen carefully to each question and to answer accordingly. In nearly all cases, the witness sees what is developing and has little difficulty coping with the attorney's questions. Moreover, most lawyers are not very good at hiding the ball, and the technique is not used too often.

UNDERMINING THE EXPERT'S ASSUMPTIONS

One of the most effective cross-examination techniques is to commit the expert witness to the facts and assumptions that support the expert's opinion, and then dispute one or more of those facts or assumptions. Consider, for example, a case in which a physician testifies on direct examination that a child experienced vaginal penetration. The cross-examiner begins by committing the doctor to the facts and assumptions underlying the opinion. The attorney says, "So, doctor, your opinion is based exclusively on the history, the physical examination, and on what the child told you. Is that correct?" "And there is nothing else you relied on to form your opinion. Is that correct?" The attorney commits the doctor to a specific set of facts and assumptions so that when the attorney disputes those facts and assumptions, the doctor's opinion cannot be justified on some other basis.

Once the cross-examiner pins down the basis of the doctor's opinion, he or she attacks the opinion by disputing one or more of the facts or assumptions supporting it. The attorney might ask the doctor whether the doctor's opinion would change if certain facts were different. The attorney might press the doctor to acknowledge alternative explanations for the doctor's conclusion. The attorney might ask the doctor whether other experts might come to a different conclusion based on the same facts. Finally, the cross-examiner might confront the doctor with a hypothetical question that favors the examiner's client. Chadwick (1990) writes that it is "common to encounter hypothetic questions based on hypotheses that are extremely unlikely, and the [expert] witness may need to point out the unlikelihood" (p. 967).

Rather than attack the doctor's assumptions during cross-examination itself, the attorney may limit cross-examination to pinning the doctor down to a limited set of facts and assumptions, and then, when the doctor has left the witness stand, offer evidence to disprove those facts and assumptions.

It is useful to think of expert testimony as a stool with three legs. The legs of the stool are the facts and assumptions supporting the expert's opinion. The cross-examiner tries to knock one of those legs away, so that the testimony comes tumbling down. With this technique of cross-examination in mind, the importance of an expert's preparing before setting foot in the courtroom is clear. The professional must possess a thorough knowledge of the facts of the case, and must be confident in the inferences, assumptions, and conclusions he or she draws from the facts.

IMPEACHING THE EXPERT
WITH A "LEARNED TREATISE"

The judge may allow a cross-examining attorney to undermine an expert's credibility by confronting the expert with authoritative books or articles that contradict the expert's opinion. The rules on impeachment with "learned treatises" vary from state to state, and professionals should discuss the learned treatise rule with any attorney who asks them to testify. The professional can prepare in advance for this type of impeachment by keeping up with the literature.

RAISING THE POSSIBILITY OF BIAS

As explained earlier, testimony from biased and partial witnesses is open to question, and the cross-examiner is permitted to inquire about bias. With an expert medical witness, for example, questioning about bias might proceed as follows:

Attorney: You met with the district attorney prior to testifying today, didn't you, doctor?

Witness: Yes.

Attorney: And during that meeting you discussed the testimony you gave on direct examination today, didn't you?

Witness: Yes.

Attorney: Now, doctor, you work at Children's Hospital, don't you?

Witness: Yes.

Attorney: You work in the child abuse unit of the pediatrics department, don't you?

Witness: Yes, that's correct.

Attorney: And you regularly perform evaluations at the request of the district attorney, don't you, doctor?

Witness: Yes, some of my work is for the district attorney's office.

Attorney: You often testify for the prosecution in child abuse cases, don't you, doctor?

Witness: Yes.

Attorney: Thank you, doctor. I have no further questions.

Notice that the attorney did not ask the final question. The attorney did not say, "So, doctor, because of your close working relationship with the district attorney's office, you are biased in favor of the prosecution, aren't you?" The attorney knows the doctor will say no to such a question, so the attorney simply raises the possibility of bias, and waits until closing argument to remind the jury of the doctor's relationship with the district attorney's office, "a relationship, ladies and gentlemen of the jury, that is just a bit too cozy."

In the foregoing cross-examination, the attorney intimated that the expert did something wrong by meeting with the prosecutor to discuss the expert's testimony. Quite the contrary—there is nothing improper in an expert's meeting with the attorney who asks him or her to testify, and there is nothing wrong with discussing what will be said in court. Chadwick (1990) aptly observes that "face-to-face conferences between . . . attorneys and [expert witnesses] are always desirable, and rarely impossible" (p. 963).

In an effort to raise questions about an expert witness's objectivity, is the cross-examiner allowed to ask whether the *expert* was a victim of child abuse? It is not illogical to suggest that victimization clouds the objectivity of some individuals. Nevertheless, this question should almost never be permitted. Such cross-examination entails a massive invasion of the expert's privacy. The psychological literature does not support the conclusion that victimization leads to impaired objectivity. Permitting such cross-examination would discourage professionals from providing expert testimony. Finally, the nexus—if there is one—between victimization and bias is simply too tenuous to merit such significant intrusion into private matters.

If the cross-examiner presses the issue, he or she should be required to establish a specific connection between victimization and impaired objectivity. For example, an expert's testimony may provide clues that suggest bias.

The cross-examiner can be expected to argue that the objectivity of at least a few experts is clouded by victimization, and the cross-examiner is entitled to find out whether this expert is among the few. The only effective way to find out is to ask. In response, it can be argued that, absent some specific evidence of bias, an expert's personal life history is not sufficiently related to bias to warrant *any* inquiry. (For legal arguments against allowing inquiry into the expert's personal history, see Myers, 1992.)

CONCLUSION

Cross-examination is usually not a pleasant experience, but in our system of justice, cross-examination is vitally important. Thus cross-examination is not easy, but it is necessary. Armed with greater understanding of the techniques and goals of cross-examination, professionals become less anxious and more effective witnesses.

❏ Reviewing Client Records in Preparation for Testifying

When a professional prepares to testify, it is often necessary for him or her to review the child's file. Such review is needed to refresh the professional's memory about important details. Some professionals take relevant files with them to court. Although review of a child's file is usually proper, a word of caution is in order. Some of the information in the file may be confidential or privileged. (See Chapter 3 for discussion of privilege and confidentiality.) If the professional uses the file to refresh his or her memory *while* testifying, the defense attorney may have the right to inspect the file, including privileged and confidential information. Thus, by referring to the child's file while testifying, the professional may unwittingly allow the defense attorney to gain access to private information that would otherwise have remained confidential.

If the professional uses the file while testifying, the defense attorney may have the right to inspect the file.

When the professional reviews the child's file *prior* to going to court, there is less chance the defense attorney will demand to see the file. Review prior to trial has some risk, however. During cross-examination of the expert witness, the defense attorney may ask whether the expert reviewed the child's file prior to testifying. If the answer is yes, the defense attorney may ask the judge to order the file produced. In most states, the judge has authority to require production of the file for review by the defense attorney.

Because of the possibility that reviewing a child's file prior to testifying could lead to disclosure of confidential or privileged information, professionals should consult with attorneys in their communities to determine in advance the best practice regarding file review.

❏ Limitations on Cross-Examination

The right to cross-examine is important, but it is not unlimited. Judges have authority to control cross-examination. The judge may prohibit questions that are unduly embarrassing for the witness or another person (Federal Rules of Evidence 611(a)). In the context of child abuse litigation, the nature of the case often makes it necessary for the cross-examiner to delve into sensitive or embarrassing issues, and judges respect the attorney's need to ask such questions. However, the judge may instruct the attorney to refrain from questions that are designed to harass or annoy witnesses.

❏ Special Accommodations
for Child Witnesses

Ask a young child to define *court,* and the child is likely to say, "It's a place to play basketball" (Saywitz, 1989). Many children are confused about the goings-on in court and about the people who work there (Saywitz, Jaenicke, & Camparo, 1990). One bewildered 5-year-old remarked that "he thought he was in a police station and that the robed judge was a karate expert" (*State v. Phelps,* 1985, p. 453). Fortunately, steps are being taken to make testifying less frightening and confusing for children (Saywitz & Snyder, in press). For example, most judges permit a young child to have a supportive adult nearby while the child testifies (Myers, 1992). Judges and attorneys are increasingly sensitive to the developmental and linguistic differences between adults and children, and to the need to provide special accommodations for children.

For many children the most traumatic aspect of testifying is facing the adult accused of abusing them (Flin, Bull, Boon, & Knox, 1992; Goodman et al., in press; Whitcomb et al., 1991). Some children simply cannot do it. Others are able to sit in the witness chair, but have difficulty talking. For some children, the best way to elicit their testimony is to allow them to testify away from the defendant. For example, most states have laws that allow selected children to testify from a separate room. The child's voice and image appear on a television monitor placed in the courtroom. In criminal cases, however, witnesses generally must testify in the physical presence of the defendant. The Sixth Amendment of the U.S. Constitution guarantees defendants the right to face-to-face confrontation with witnesses against them. The Constitution does not require that witnesses actually look at the defendant, but the opportunity for face-to-face confrontation is an important constitutional right (*Coy v. Iowa*, 1988).

Fortunately, in 1990 the U.S. Supreme Court ruled that the Sixth Amendment right to confront accusatory witnesses is not absolute (*Maryland v. Craig*, 1990). At times, children may be spared the trauma of face-to-face confrontation with the defendant. The Supreme Court made clear, however, that there can be no generalized presumption that all, most, or even very many children can be spared face-to-face confrontation. For example, there can be no presumption that children below a specified age should be protected in this way. Face-to-face confrontation remains the norm, and exceptions must be rare and must be made on a case-by-case basis.

When a prosecutor asks a judge to allow a child to testify away from the defendant, the prosecutor must convince the judge that dispensing with face-to-face confrontation is needed to protect the child from serious emotional trauma. The distress experienced by the child must be more than the nervousness, excitement, and reluctance exhibited by many witnesses. Face-to-face confrontation with the defendant must pose a risk of serious psychological trauma. Furthermore, the judge must find that the source of the trauma is the defendant, not the courtroom.

In some cases, professionals familiar with a child are asked to provide expert testimony on whether the child will be traumatized by face-to-face confrontation. For example, the child's psychotherapist may have useful information to share with the judge. Legal research concerning expert testimony provided by children's therapists raises the disturbing possibility that some expert testimony on the trauma of face-to-face confrontation is little more than speculation. Frankly, in some cases the therapist's testimony appears to reflect more about the therapist's *own* anxiety about being a witness than it does about the child. In other cases, the therapist's testimony seems based on an unspoken *presumption* that face-to-face confrontation is seriously harmful for children. This is precisely the kind of presumption the Supreme Court said violates the constitutional rights of defendants. Although psychological research indicates that face-to-face confrontation is traumatic for some children (Goodman et al., in press), a defendant's right to confront witnesses cannot be dispensed with on the basis of presumptions.

As an example of the kind of vague expert testimony that is not very helpful, consider the following testimony from a child's therapist: "I believe it would be very difficult for the child to sit in the same room with the defendant and discuss the abuse. The child would probably stop talking and would withdraw and curl up." This testimony is too conclusory. The expert's conclusion may help a little, but the judge needs more than conclusions. What the judge needs are *specific* facts and data that support the conclusion that testifying will be traumatic.

The most helpful expert testimony about the trauma of face-to-face confrontation provides specific information that the judge can use to reach a conclusion about the effect of face-to-face confrontation on a particular child. Consider the following types of information.

1. *Predicting future behavior from past behavior.* One way to predict how a child will react to face-to-face confrontation is to find out whether the child has faced the defendant in other settings. If so, and the child fared poorly, the professional has concrete data on which to base an opinion about the likelihood of trauma. For example, if a child was abused by a stranger, the child may have gone to the police station to pick the defendant out of a lineup. Did the child freeze at the sight of the defendant? Did the child show signs of serious emotional distress? In an intrafamilial abuse case, the professional should find out whether

the child visited with the alleged perpetrator, and, if so, how the visits went. If the child testified in the defendant's presence at a preliminary hearing or some other proceeding, the professional should find out what the child's reaction was to face-to-face confrontation.

2. *The child's reaction when the subject of testifying comes up at home or in therapy.* If the subject of testifying has come up in therapy, at home, or in other settings, how did the child react? In one case, the child had a serious ulcer, and every time testifying was mentioned the child cried.

3. *Signs of psychological distress as the date for testifying approaches.* Some children regress and experience other symptoms of psychological distress as the day for testifying approaches. Parents observe the child's worsening condition, and can provide this information to the judge. In some cases, the best evidence of the need to dispense with face-to-face confrontation is a combination of expert testimony from the child's therapist and lay testimony from the child's parents.

4. *The child's mental health status.* If a child has serious mental health problems that could be exacerbated by face-to-face confrontation, the professional should inform the judge.

5. *Sources and severity of the child's fear of the defendant.* The professional can describe the impact of any threats made by the defendant. The professional can help the judge understand that because of the child's immaturity, threats that an adult would not take seriously may paralyze a child. For example, suppose the defendant threatened the child that if she said anything, a terrible monster would slither out of her closet at night and devour her and her parents. An adult would dismiss such a threat, but to a young child this type of threat may be very real. The professional can help the judge put the defendant's threats in developmental perspective.

6. *Impact of face-to-face confrontation on the child's ability to communicate effectively.* If the professional has concrete evidence that face-to-face confrontation would impair a child's ability to communicate fully and accurately, the judge should be informed.

7. *Lack of any psychological test to determine trauma.* Professionals should remember that the judge is a layperson who may believe some psychological test could be given to a child to determine whether face-to-face confrontation will traumatize the child. The professional can help by informing the judge that there are no psychological tests that predict whether face-to-face confrontation will harm a child.

7

Lawsuits Against Professionals Working With Abused and Neglected Children

Professionals working with abused and neglected children dread the thought of being sued, so before presenting this discussion, a word of reassurance is appropriate: Lawsuits against professionals are uncommon, and when professionals are sued, the lawsuits are usually unsuccessful.

Although most professionals will never be sued, the possibility cannot be ignored, and this chapter provides a brief overview of the kinds of lawsuits that are brought against professionals working with abused and neglected children. The next section focuses on lawsuits against professionals in private practice; this is followed by discussion of lawsuits against professionals employed by the government.

176

❏ Lawsuits Against Professionals in Private Practice

Medical and mental health professionals in private practice cannot rule out the possibility of being sued by angry parents. This section discusses two types of suits. First, professionals are occasionally sued as a result of their decision to report suspected maltreatment to CPS. Second, professionals providing treatment to children are occasionally sued for failure to obtain informed consent, failure to consult other professionals, improper disclosure of confidential information, or professional malpractice.

LAWSUITS RELATED TO THE REPORTING LAWS

Chapter 4 describes laws that require professionals to report suspected child abuse and neglect. In rare cases, professionals are sued for decisions they make about reporting.

Failure to Report
Suspected Abuse or Neglect

In a few cases, professionals who failed to report suspected maltreatment have been sued. For example, in *Landeros v. Flood* (1976), the California Supreme Court ruled that a physician who failed to diagnose battered child syndrome and report to CPS could be sued for medical malpractice. In *Landeros*, an 11-month-old baby was taken to the hospital with injuries indicative of battered child syndrome. Dr. Flood examined the child and released her to her mother and stepfather, after which she was abused again. The child sued Dr. Flood for the injuries she suffered *after* she was returned to her abusers. The child's suit alleged that the injuries would not have happened if Dr. Flood had diagnosed battered child syndrome and reported to CPS. Thus failure to discover and report abuse or neglect that would be discovered by competent professionals can lead to a lawsuit.

Laws in several states impose civil liability on professionals who fail to report suspected abuse (e.g., Arkansas Code of 1987 Annotated § 12-12-503 [b]; Colorado Revised Statutes, 1986, § 19-10-104[4][b];

Montana Code Annotated, 1989, § 41-3-207[1]; McKinney's New York Social Services Law § 420[2]). Nearly all states impose criminal penalties on professionals who knowingly fail to report suspected child abuse (Myers & Peters, 1987, pp. 210-211). A small number of professionals have been prosecuted for failing to report abuse they knew about.

Lawsuits for Reporting
Suspected Abuse or Neglect

In a few cases, professionals have been sued *for* reporting suspected abuse. The outcome of such suits usually depends on how the judge interprets the portion of the reporting law that grants immunity from lawsuits to professionals who report suspected abuse. In the case of *Maples v. Siddiqui* (1990), a physician was sued for malpractice. The child was an infant with malnutrition caused by a medical problem. The doctor misdiagnosed the child's malnutrition as nonorganic failure to thrive caused by poor parenting. As a result of this misdiagnosis, the child was temporarily placed in foster care. Further testing revealed the medical explanation for the child's condition, and the child was returned to the parents. The angry parents sued the doctor and claimed that the doctor committed malpractice when he misdiagnosed the child's condition. The court ruled that even if the doctor was negligent, he acted in good faith, and was entitled to the immunity granted by the Iowa reporting law.

As long as professionals act competently and in good faith, they are entitled to immunity from suit when they report suspected abuse or neglect, even if the report turns out to be unfounded.

Defamation of Character

In some circumstances, a person who says untruthful things about someone else can be sued for defamation of character, commonly called libel or slander. In several cases, professionals who reported suspected child abuse were sued by parents who claimed that the reports were untrue and defamatory. In a New York case, a physician informed a child's parent that he would have to report his suspicion of abuse to CPS. The parent sued the doctor, but the court ruled against the parent. The court wrote, "If a professional has made or intends to make a report of suspected child abuse, he will frequently find it necessary and should feel free to discuss the report and the suspicions necessitating it with those directly concerned. . . . he should not do so at the risk of exposing himself to civil liability" (*Salter v. Larsen*, 1987).

Additional Protections Provided by Some Reporting Laws

Several state reporting laws extend immunity to designated professionals who take children into emergency protective custody (*Lehman v. Stephens*, 1986; Colorado Revised Statutes, 1986, § 19-10-110; Utah Code Annotated, 1987, § 78-3b-9). Some reporting laws provide immunity from suit for professionals who cooperate with the CPS investigation (Vernon's Annotated Missouri Statutes, 1983, § 210.135), or who testify in judicial proceedings arising out of a report (Florida Statutes Annotated, 1976, § 827.07(9); Vernon's Annotated Missouri Statutes, 1983, § 210.135).

In two decisions from California, the court ruled that the immunity afforded by the California reporting law extends beyond the initial report, and includes follow-up communications between the reporter and investigating agencies (*Ferraro v. Chadwick*, 1990; *Thomas v. Chadwick*, 1990).

LIABILITY OF PROFESSIONALS PROVIDING MEDICAL AND MENTAL HEALTH TREATMENT

When the focus shifts from the reporting laws to treatment, lawsuits arise in several ways.

Failure to Obtain Informed Consent to Treatment

As a general rule, children are not competent to consent to treatment, and parents provide the necessary consent. When a parent is suspected of abuse, however, the consent issue becomes complicated. When an emergency exists, most states authorize treatment without parental consent. Some states authorize minors to consent to certain types of medical and mental health treatment. Consent should normally be obtained from the adult who is legally responsible for the child.

Failure to Consult Other Professionals

Professional liability can be based on failure to consult other professionals when consultation is indicated. For example, a psychotherapist may need to refer a client to a physician if signs of organicity appear.

Professional Malpractice

Negligent performance of psychotherapy can constitute malpractice (Furrow, 1980). A professional commits malpractice when the professional's conduct falls below the standard of care required of professionals providing similar services.

Unauthorized Disclosure of
Confidential Information About Clients

Professionals have an obligation to protect confidential information about clients, and to prevent improper disclosure of such information. Generally, the consent of the client is required to release confidential information. Improper release of confidential information can lead to a lawsuit (Gutheil & Appelbaum, 1982). (See Chapter 3 for discussion of release of confidential information.)

❏ Lawsuits Against Professionals
Employed by the Government[1]

In the England of King Arthur, the government and its employees could not be sued. The government enjoyed sovereign immunity from suit. The legal phrase for this situation is "The king can do no wrong." The doctrine of sovereign immunity made the journey to

America, and until the twentieth century, the state, its political sub-
divisions, and government employees enjoyed complete immunity
from suit. As state and local governments grew, more and more people
were injured by government employees. Because of sovereign immunity, however, neither the government nor its employees could
be sued. Gradually, the doctrine of complete sovereign immunity
fell into disfavor, and today, all states permit some lawsuits against
the state, city, and county governments, and their employees.

As the sovereign immunity of state and local governments was
pared back, lawsuits against the government increased in state courts.
At the same time, an increase occurred in the number of lawsuits
brought in federal court against cities, counties, and their employees. Most of the lawsuits in federal court are filed under a federal
law commonly known as Section 1983 (United States Code, Title 42,
§ 1983). An individual can sue under Section 1983 if an employee of
a state, city, town, or county deprives the citizen of rights guaranteed by the U.S. Constitution or by federal laws.

Lawsuits in state and federal court against child welfare professionals and their agency employers usually fall into one of the following categories.

INJURIES TO CHILDREN

State law requires CPS agencies to investigate reports of suspected child abuse and neglect and to protect vulnerable children.
Several courts have found that a special legal relationship exists
between CPS and a child who is the subject of a report of suspected
abuse (*Turner v. District of Columbia*, 1987; *Department of Health & Rehabilitation Services v. Yamuni*, 1988). This special relationship imposes
a duty on CPS professionals to act competently. A caseworker whose
incompetence leads to a child's injury could be sued.

FAILURE TO REPORT
SUSPECTED ABUSE OR NEGLECT

The obligation to report suspected child abuse and neglect is
shared by all professionals who interact with children, including professionals employed by the government. Situations arise in which

child welfare professionals know of abuse but fail to report it. Failure to report may lead to a lawsuit.

FAILURE TO INVESTIGATE A REPORT

Although there are times when it is difficult to investigate a report of suspected abuse or neglect, some failure to investigate is attributable to negligence (*Brodie v. Summit County Children Services Board*, 1990). A child who suffers abuse that could have been prevented by a competent investigation may sue.

FAILURE TO CONDUCT
AN ADEQUATE INVESTIGATION

An investigation may be so inadequate that the investigating professional is negligent. For example, if the investigation does not begin in a timely manner, if the child is not observed or interviewed, if collateral sources of information are not checked out, or if a necessary medical examination is not requested, a lawsuit may follow.

FAILURE TO REMOVE A CHILD
OR TO PROTECT A CHILD LEFT IN THE HOME

> *The decision to remove a child from the home may lead to a lawsuit, but so may a decision not to remove a child.*

The decision to remove a child from the home may lead to a lawsuit, but so may a decision not to remove a child. The decisive issue in both situations is whether the professional exercised reasonable judgment under the circumstances existing at the time. One benchmark of reasonable judgment is whether the professional complied with applicable professional standards for decision making. A professional who exercises reasonable judgment under the circumstances cannot be sued successfully just because the professional's judgment turns out to be wrong (*Callahan v. Iowa*, 1986; *Vosburg v. Department of Social Services*, 1989).

In 1989, the U.S. Supreme Court decided the case of *DeShaney v. Winnebago County Department of Social Services*. In the *DeShaney* case, CPS knew that young Joshua DeShaney's father might harm him, but decided to leave Joshua at home. Tragically, Joshua's father inflicted irreparable brain damage on his son. Joshua was not in the custody of the state at the time of his injuries. Joshua sued CPS in federal court for failure to protect him. Joshua claimed that CPS violated his rights under the U.S. Constitution and Section 1983. The U.S. Supreme Court rejected Joshua's lawsuit and ruled that the U.S. Constitution does not impose an affirmative duty on the government to protect private citizens from each other unless those citizens are in government custody.

After the *DeShaney* case, a child who is not in state custody when abuse occurs will have difficulty using Section 1983 to sue the government or its employees. However, the Supreme Court's *DeShaney* decision deals *only* with suits under Section 1983. Nothing in the *DeShaney* case forecloses suits that do not rely on Section 1983. For example, the *DeShaney* decision does not foreclose a suit in state court alleging that failure to remove a child from a dangerous home was negligent. Furthermore, in *DeShaney*, the U.S. Supreme Court did not decide whether a child who is in state custody when abuse occurs may sue under Section 1983. For example, if a child is abused in foster care, a Section 1983 action against the agency responsible for supervising the foster home may succeed (*Artist M. v. Johnson*, 1989; *Taylor v. Ledbetter*, 1987).

FAILURE TO PROTECT CHILDREN IN FOSTER CARE OR OTHER OUT-OF-HOME SETTINGS

Once the government takes custody of a child and places the child in foster care or some other out-of-home setting, the government is responsible for the child's safety. Failure to protect the child can lead to liability.

VIOLATION OF PARENTAL RIGHTS

The U.S. Constitution protects the right of parents to the care, custody, and control of their children. Unwarranted government intervention into the privacy of the family can violate the constitutional rights of parents, and can lead to lawsuits against professionals (*Achterhof v. Selvaggio*, 1989). Angry parents have alleged a rather remarkable variety of wrongdoing by professionals, including defamation, assault and battery, intentional infliction of emotional distress, alienation of affection, and even racketeering. For the most part, lawsuits claiming violation of parental rights are unsuccessful (*Martin v. Weld County*, 1979; *Russell v. Texas Department of Human Resources*, 1988).

Lest the thought of being sued tempt the reader to think twice about a career in child protection, it is important to note that government professionals still have considerable protection from liability. This protection comes from several sources. All child abuse reporting laws grant immunity to persons who report child abuse in good faith. Some reporting statutes extend immunity to persons who cooperate with child protection investigations and testify in related judicial proceedings. More significantly, a number of reporting laws extend immunity to government employees for their child protection activities. This immunity is not absolute, but as long as government employees act in good faith, they are immune from most types of civil liability. Some child welfare activities, such as the decision to file a petition in juvenile court, may enjoy absolute immunity from suit.

In addition to providing qualified immunity from most types of lawsuits, many states protect government employees against the financial consequences of being sued. For example, many states place a cap on damages recoverable in lawsuits against public employees. Thus, rather than facing multimillion-dollar judgments, public employees may face judgments in the hundreds of thousands of dollars. Of course, even such amounts are beyond the means of most professionals. Therefore, many states have laws that allow money judgments against government employees to be paid by the government. And finally, because most government employees cannot afford to pay for lawyers to defend them, many states provide free legal representation to their employees.

❑ Conclusion

Working with abused and neglected children and their parents is difficult in the best of circumstances. The possibility of being sued adds yet another layer of worry to an already heavy load. Nevertheless, the dedicated professionals working in this field willingly accept the small risk of a lawsuit because they know the children they serve are worth the risk.

❑ Note

1. This section is based on an article by Robert Horowitz, J.D., associate director of the American Bar Association's Center on Children and the Law. The article, "Civil Liability of Government Child Welfare Professionals" (1990), is reproduced here in modified form with Mr. Horowitz's permission.

Appendix:
Sample Court Order
to Protect Access to Videotapes

This stipulation and order are based on documents prepared by the district attorney's office in _____.

THE PEOPLE OF THE STATE OF _____)No.:
)
                Plaintiff,   )Hearing Date:
)Time:
       vs.   )Dept.:
)
)STIPULATION AND ORDER
_____, Defendant.   )RE: DISCOVERY
_____)

IT IS HEREBY STIPULATED by and between the parties that the District Attorney make available to defendant(s) one copy [sometimes referred to as the defense copy] of each videotaped statement made by a witness in this case to any law enforcement officer, child protective services employee, or representative of the _____ Office, on the following terms and conditions:

1. The cost of copying the tape(s) shall be borne by the defense.

2. The tape(s) shall not be used for any purpose other than to prepare for the defense of _____ in this case.

3. The parties understand and specifically agree that the tape(s) supplied to the defense shall not be publicly exhibited, shown, displayed, used for educational, research, or demonstration purposes, or used in any other fashion, except in judicial proceedings in the above-entitled case.

4. No copies of the tape(s) provided to the defense shall be made by the defendant, the defendant's attorney, investigator, expert, or any other representative or agent of the defendant or their employees. No transcripts of the tape(s) may be prepared.

5. The identity of any expert retained by the defense (whether the expert will testify or not) shall be disclosed in camera to the court. This information shall be kept sealed in the court file and will not be disclosed to anyone except by court order.

6. Before turning over the defense copy of any videotape released under this stipulation to an expert, the defense shall obtain from the expert a declaration signed under penalty of perjury that the expert has read this Stipulation and Order and understands the conditions under which the tape(s) is being received by the expert, and that a violation of the order made on this stipulation shall subject the expert to a contempt citation. This declaration shall be kept sealed in the court file and shall not be disclosed to anyone except by court order.

7. When a final disposition is reached in this case, the defense copy shall be returned to the District Attorney, and the erased videocassette or -cassettes, or another blank cassette, shall be returned to the defendant.

8. Counsel appearing ex parte and presenting this order for the court's signature shall have so notified all other counsel of record in this proceeding.

9. Any violation of the order based on this stipulation will result in a contempt citation against the violator.

10. This stipulation and the order made thereon shall be continuing in nature, and shall apply to the case whether pending in Municipal or Superior Court or on appeal.

Dated: _____

_____
DEPUTY DISTRICT ATTORNEY

Dated: _____

_____
Attorney at Law,
Attorney for _____

Dated: _____

_____
Attorney at Law,
Attorney for_____

ORDER

IT IS SO ORDERED.

Dated: _____

_____
JUDGE OF THE _____ COURT

References

Achterhof v. Selvaggio, 886 F.2d 826 (6th Cir. 1989).

Adoption of Abigail, 499 N.E.2d 1234 (Mass. Ct. App. 1986).

American Academy of Child and Adolescent Psychiatry. (1988). Guidelines for the clinical evaluation of child and adolescent sexual abuse. *American Journal of Child and Adolescent Psychiatry, 27,* 655-657.

American Academy of Child and Adolescent Psychiatry. (1990). *Guidelines for the clinical evaluation of child and adolescent sexual abuse.* Washington, DC: Author.

American Medical Association. (1989). *Principles of medical ethics.* Washington, DC: Author.

American Nurses Association. (1985). *Code for nurses.* Washington, DC: Author.

American Professional Society on the Abuse of Children. (1990). *Guidelines for psychosocial evaluation of suspected sexual abuse in young children.* Chicago: Author.

American Psychiatric Association. (1987). *Diagnostic and statistical manual of mental disorders* (3rd ed.). Washington, DC: Author.

American Psychological Association. (1981). Ethical principles of psychologists. *American Psychologist, 36,* 633-638.

Artist M. v. Johnson, 726 F. Supp. 690 (N.D. Ill. 1989).

Bays, J. (1990). Substance abuse and child abuse: The impact of addiction on the child. *Pediatric Clinics of North America, 37,* 881-904.

Bays, J., & Chadwick, D. L. (in press). Medical diagnosis of the sexually abused child. *Child Abuse & Neglect.*

Beitchman, J. H., Zucker, K. J., Hood, J. E., DaCosta, G. A., & Akman, D. (1991). A review of the short-term effects of child sexual abuse. *Child Abuse & Neglect, 15,* 537-556.

Berliner, L. (1988). Deciding whether a child has been sexually abused. In B. Nicholson & J. Bulkley (Eds.), *Sexual abuse allegations in custody and visitation cases* (pp. 48-69). Washington, DC: American Bar Association.

Berliner, L., & Conte, J. R. (in press). Sexual abuse evaluations: Conceptual and empirical obstacles. *Child Abuse & Neglect.*

Black, B. (1988). A unified theory of scientific evidence. *Fordham Law Review, 56,* 595-695.

Black v. Gray, 540 A.2d 431 (Del. 1988).

Boat, B. W., & Everson, M. D. (1988). Interviewing young children with anatomical dolls. *Child Welfare, 67,* 337-352.

Boat, B. W., Everson, M. D., & Holland, J. (1990). Maternal perceptions of nonabused young children's behaviors after the children's exposure to anatomical dolls. *Child Welfare, 69,* 389-400.

Briere, J., & Runtz, M. (1990). Differential adult symptomatology associated with three types of child abuse histories. *Child Abuse & Neglect, 14,* 357-364.

Brigham, J. C., Van Verst, M., & Bothwell, R. K. (1986). Accuracy of children's eyewitness identifications in a field setting. *Basic and Applied Social Psychology, 7,* 295-306.

Broderick v. King's Way Assembly of God Church, 808 P.2d 1211 (Alaska 1991).

Brodie v. Summit County Children Services Board, 554 N.E.2d 1301 (Ohio 1990).

Brown, M. (1926). *Legal psychology.* Indianapolis: Bobbs-Merrill.

Browne, A., & Finkelhor, D. (1986). Impact of child sexual abuse: A review of the research. *Psychological Bulletin, 99,* 66-77.

Burgess, A. W., & Holmstrom, L. L. (1974). Rape trauma syndrome. *American Journal of Psychiatry, 131,* 981-986.

Bussey, K. (1992). Lying and truthfulness: Children's definitions, standards, and evaluation reactions. *Child Development, 63,* 129-137.

Caffey, J. (1974). The whiplash shaken infant syndrome: Manual shaking by the extremities with whiplash-induced intracranial and intraocular bleeding, linked with residual permanent brain damage and mental retardation. *Pediatrics, 54,* 396-403.

Callahan v. Iowa, 385 N.W.2d 533 (Iowa 1986).

Ceci, S. J. (1991). Some overarching issues in the children's suggestibility debate. In J. Doris (Ed.), *The suggestibility of children's recollections* (pp. 1-9). Washington, DC: American Psychological Association.

Ceci, S. J., Ross, D. F., & Toglia, M. P. (1987). Age differences in suggestibility: Narrowing the uncertainties. In S. J. Ceci, M. P. Toglia, & D. F. Ross (Eds.), *Children's eyewitness memory* (pp. 79-91). New York: Springer-Verlag.

Chadwick, D. L. (1989). [Review of *Accusations of child sexual abuse*]. *Journal of the American Medical Association, 261,* 3035.

Chadwick, D. L. (1990). Preparation for court testimony in child abuse cases. *Pediatric Clinics of North America, 37,* 955-970.

Chadwick, D. L., Chin, S., Salerno, C., Landsverk, J., & Kitchen, L. (1991). Deaths from falls in children: How far is fatal? *Journal of Trauma, 31,* 1353-1355.

Chadwick, D. L., & Myers, J. E. B. (1992). *Inflicted head injury in children: Research steps toward greater accuracy of diagnosis.* Unpublished manuscript.

Cicchetti, D., & Nurcombe, B. (Eds.). (1991). Defining psychological maltreatment [Special issue]. *Development and Psychopathology, 3*(1).

Claussen, A. H., & Crittenden, P. M. (1991). Physical and psychological maltreatment: Relations among types of maltreatment. *Child Abuse & Neglect, 15,* 5-18.

Coleman, L., & Clancy, P. E. (1990). False allegations of child sexual abuse: Why is it happening? What can we do? *Criminal Justice, 5*(3), 14-20, 43-47.

Commonwealth v. Dunkle, 602 A.2d 830 (Pa. 1992).

Commonwealth v. Gallagher, 547 A.2d 355 (Pa. 1988).

Commonwealth v. Mamay, 553 N.E.2d 945 (Mass. 1990).

Conte, J. R., Sorenson, E., Fogarty, L., & Dalla Rosa, J. (1991). Evaluating children's reports of sexual abuse: Results from a survey of professionals. *American Journal of Orthopsychiatry, 61,* 428-437.

Corwin, D. L. (1988). Early diagnosis of child sexual abuse: Diminishing the lasting effects. In G. E. Wyatt & G. J. Powell (Eds.), *Lasting effects of child sexual abuse* (pp. 251-269). Newbury Park, CA: Sage.

Cosgrove, J. M., & Patterson, C. J. (1977). Plans and the development of listener skills. *Developmental Psychology, 13,* 557-564.

Coy v. Iowa, 487 U.S. 1012 (1988).

Custody of a Minor, 379 N.E.2d 1053 (Mass. 1978).

Davies, D., & Montegna, D. (1990). Strategies for coping with avoidant children. *Advisor, 3*(2), 8.

Dent, H. R. (1990). Experimental studies of interviewing child witnesses. In J. Doris (Ed.), *Suggestibility of children's recollections* (pp. 138-146). Washington, DC: American Psychological Association.

Department of Health and Rehabilitation Services v. Yamuni, 529 So.2d 258 (Fla. 1988).

DeShaney v. Winnebago County Department of Social Services, 489 U.S. 189 (1989).

Dickson, W. (Ed.). (1981). *Children's oral communications skills.* New York: Academic Press.

D.M. v. State, 515 P.2d 1234 (Alaska 1973).

Dorland's Illustrated Medical Dictionary. (1981). Philadelphia: W. B. Saunders.

Duquette, D. N. (1990). *Advocating for the child in protection proceedings: A handbook for lawyers and court appointed special advocates.* Lexington, MA: Lexington.

Dykes, L. J. (1986). The whiplash shaken infant syndrome: What has been learned? *Child Abuse & Neglect, 10,* 211-221.

Edwards, L. P. (1987). The relationships of family and juvenile courts in child abuse cases. *Santa Clara Law Review, 27,* 201-278.

Everson, M. D., & Boat, B. W. (1990). Sexualized doll play among young children: Implications for the use of anatomical dolls in sexual abuse evaluations. *Journal of the American Academy of Child and Adolescent Psychiatry, 29,* 736-742.

Faller, K. C., (1988). Criteria for judging the credibility of children's statements about their sexual abuse. *Child Welfare, 67,* 389-401.

Faller, K. C. (1990). *Understanding child sexual maltreatment.* Newbury Park, CA: Sage.

Faller, K. C., & Corwin, D. L. (in press). Children's interview statements and behaviors: Role in identifying sexually abused children. *Child Abuse & Neglect.*

Famularo, R. A., Kinscherff, R., Burnshaft, D., Spivak, G., & Fenton, T. (1989). Parental compliance to court-ordered treatment interventions in cases of child maltreatment. *Child Abuse & Neglect, 13,* 507-514.

Famularo, R. A., Stone, K., Barnum, R., & Wharton, R. (1986). Alcoholism and severe child maltreatment. *American Journal of Orthopsychiatry, 56,* 481-485.

Felthous, A. R. (1989). The ever confusing jurisprudence of the psychotherapist's duty to protect. *Journal of Psychiatry and Law, 17,* 575-594.

Ferraro v. Chadwick, 270 Cal. Rptr. 379 (Ct. App. 1990).

Finkelhor, D. (1979). *Sexually victimized children.* New York: Free Press.

Finkelhor, D. (1990). Is child abuse overreported? The data rebut arguments for less intervention. *Public Welfare, 48,* 22-29, 46-47.

Fivush, R. (in press). Developmental perspectives on autobiographical recall. In G. S. Goodman & B. L. Bottoms (Eds.), *Understanding and improving children's testimony.* New York: Guilford.

Fivush, R., Gray, J. T., & Fromhoff, F. A. (1987). Two-year-olds talk about the past. *Cognitive Development, 2,* 393-409.

Fivush, R., & Hamond, N. R. (1990). Autobiographical memory across the preschool years: Toward reconceptualizing childhood amnesia. In R. Fivush & J. A. Hudson (Eds.), *Knowing and remembering in young children* (pp. 223-248). New York: Cambridge University Press.

Fivush, R., Hamond, N. R., Harsch, N., Singer, N., & Wolf, A. (1991). Content and consistency in young children's autobiographical recall. *Discourse Processes, 14,* 373-388.

Flavell, J. H. (1981). Cognitive monitoring. In W. Dickson (Ed.), *Children's oral communication skills* (pp. 35-60). New York: Academic Press.

Flavell, J. H., Speer, J. R., Green, F. L., & August, D. L. (1981). The development of comprehension monitoring and knowledge about communication. *Monographs of the Society for Research on Child Development, 46*(Serial No. 192).

Flin, R., Boon, J., Knox, A., & Bull, R. (1992). The effect of a five-month delay on children's and adults' eyewitness memory. *British Journal of Psychology, 83.*

Flin, R., Bull, R., Boon, J., & Knox, A. (1992). *Child witnesses in Scottish criminal trials.* Manuscript submitted for publication.

Fortescue, J. (1660). *De laudibus legum angliae.* London.

Friedrich, W. N. (in press). Sexual victimization and sexual behavior in children. *Child Abuse & Neglect.*

Friedrich, W. N., & Grambach, P. (in press). The child sexual behavior inventory: Normative and clinical comparisons. *Psychological Assessment.*

Friedrich, W. N., Grambach, P., Broughton, D., Kruper, J., & Beilke, R. L. (1991). Normative sexual behavior in children. *Pediatrics, 88,* 456-464.

Furrow, B. (1980). *Malpractice in psychotherapy.* Lexington, MA: Lexington.

Garbarino, J., Guttmann, E., & Seeley, J. (1986). *The psychologically battered child.* San Francisco: Jossey-Bass.

Garbarino, J., & Stott, F. M. (1989). *What children can tell us.* San Francisco: Jossey-Bass.

Gardner, R. (1987a). *The parental alienation syndrome and the differentiation between fabricated and genuine child sex abuse.* Creskill, NJ: Creative Therapeutics.

Gardner, R. (1987b). *The Sex Abuse Legitimacy Scale.* Creskill, NJ: Creative Therapeutics.

Gardner, R. (1989). Differentiating between bona fide and fabricated allegations of sexual abuse of children. *Journal of the American Academy of Matrimonial Lawyers, 5,* 1-25.

Glendening v. State, 536 So.2d 212 (Fla. 1988).

Goodman, G. S. (1984). Children's testimony in historical perspective. *Journal of Social Issues, 40,* 9-31.

Goodman, G. S., & Aman, C. (1990). Children's use of anatomically detailed dolls to recount an event. *Child Development, 61,* 1859-1871.

Goodman, G. S., Bottoms, B. L., Schwartz-Kenney, B. M., & Rudy, L. (1991). Children's testimony about a stressful event: Improving children's reports. *Journal of Narrative & Life History, 1*, 69-99.

Goodman, G. S., & Clarke-Stewart, A. (1991). Suggestibility in children's testimony: Implications for child sexual abuse investigations. In J. Doris (Ed.), *The suggestibility of children's recollections* (pp. 92-105). Washington, DC: American Psychological Association.

Goodman, G. S., Hirschman, J. E., Hepps, D., & Rudy, L. (1991). Children's memory for stressful events. *Merrill-Palmer Quarterly, 37, 109-158.*

Goodman, G. S., & Reed, R. S. (1986). Age differences in eyewitness testimony. *Law & Human Behavior, 10*, 317-332.

Goodman, G. S., Rudy, L., Bottoms, B. L., & Aman, C. (1990). Children's concerns and memory: Issues of ecological validity in the study of children's eyewitness testimony. In R. Fivush & J. A. Hudson (Eds.), *Knowing and remembering in young children* (pp. 249-284). New York: Cambridge University Press.

Goodman, G. S., & Schwartz-Kenney, B. M. (in press). Why knowing a child's age is not enough: Influences of cognitive, social, and emotional factors on children's testimony. In R. Flin & H. Dent (Eds.), *Children as witnesses.* London: John Wiley.

Goodman, G. S., Taub, E. P., Jones, D. T. H., England, P., Port, L. K., Rudy, L., & Prado-Estrada, L. (in press). The emotional effects of criminal court testimony on child sexual assault victims. *Monographs of the Society for Research in Child Development.*

Goodson v. State, 566 So.2d 1142 (Miss. 1990).

Gutheil, T. G., & Appelbaum, P. S. (1982). *Clinical handbook of psychiatry and the law.* New York: McGraw-Hill.

Hall, E., Lamb, M., & Perlmutter, M. (1986). *Child psychology today.* New York: Random House.

Hamond, N. R., & Fivush, R. (1991). Memories of Mickey Mouse: Young children recount their trip to Disney World. *Cognitive Development, 6*, 433-448.

Hart, H. M., & McNaughton, J. (1958). *Evidence and inference in the law.* Washington, DC: American Academy of Arts and Sciences.

Hart, S. N., & Brassard, M. R. (1991). *Developing and validating operationally defined measures of emotional maltreatment* (NCCAN research grant addendum to final report; Grant No. HHS 90CA1216 HART).

Hart, S. N., Germain, R., & Brassard, M. R. (1987). The challenge: To better understand and combat psychological maltreatment of children and youth. In M. R. Brassard, R. Germain, & S. N. Hart (Eds.), *Psychological maltreatment of children and youth* (pp. 3-24). New York: Pergamon.

Haugaard, J. L., Reppucci, N. D., Laird, J., & Nauful, T. (1991). Children's definitions of the truth and their competency as witnesses in legal proceedings. *Law & Human Development, 15*, 253-271.

Hawkins v. McGee, 146 A. 641 (N.H. 1929).

Horowitz, R. (1990). Civil liability of government child welfare professionals. *Violence Update, 1*(4), 3, 9, 12.

Hudson, J. A. (1990). The emergence of autobiographical memory in mother-child conversation. In R. Fivush & J. A. Hudson (Eds.), *Knowing and remembering in young children* (pp. 166-196). New York: Cambridge University Press.

Hudson, J. A., & Fivush, R. (1990). Introduction: What young children remember and why. In R. Fivush & J. A. Hudson (Eds.), *Knowing and remembering in young children* (pp. 1-8). New York: Cambridge University Press.

Hudson, J. A., & Fivush, R. (1991). As time goes by: Sixth graders remember a kindergarten experience. *Applied Cognitive Psychology, 5,* 347-360.

Idaho v. Wright, 110 S.Ct. 3139 (1990).

In re Adoption of T. M., 566 A.2d 1256 (Pa. Super. 1989).

In re Amber B., 236 Cal. Rptr. 623 (1987).

In re Colin R., 493 A.2d 1083 (Md. Ct. App. 1985).

In re D.K., 245 N.W.2d 644 (1976).

In re E.G., 549 N.E.2d 322 (Ill. 1990).

In re Jamie M., 184 Cal. Rptr. 778 (1982).

In re K.S., 737 P.2d 170 (Utah 1987).

In re P.H., 783 P.2d 565 (Utah Ct. App. 1989).

In re Penelope B., 709 P.2d 1185 (Wash. 1985).

In re Winship, 397 U.S. 358 (1970).

Johnson v. State, 732 S.W.2d 817 (Ark. 1987).

Johnson, M. K., & Foley, M. A. (1984). Differentiating fact from fantasy: The reliability of children's memory. *Journal of Social Issues, 40,* 33-50.

Jones, D., & McQuiston, M. (1985). *Interviewing the sexually abused child.* Denver, CO: C. Henry Kempe National Center for the Prevention and Treatment of Child Abuse and Neglect.

Jones, D. P. H., & Krugman, R. D. (1986). Can a three-year old child bear witness to her sexual assault and attempted murder? *Child Abuse & Neglect, 10,* 253-258.

Kempe, C. H., Silverman, F. N., Steele, B. F., Droegmuller, W., & Silver, H. K. (1962). The battered-child syndrome. *Journal of the American Medical Association, 181,* 17-24.

Kendall-Tackett, K. (1991). Believing children vs. being neutral: What you think can influence your judgments about suspected victims of sexual abuse. *Advisor, 4*(3), 4.

Kit-fong Au, T. (1992). Counterfactual reasoning. In G. R. Semin & K. Fiedler (Eds.), *Language, interaction and social cognition.* London: Sage.

Kolko, D. J., & Moser, J. T. (1988). Behavioral/emotional indicators of sexual abuse in child psychiatric inpatients: A controlled comparison with physical abuse. *Child Abuse & Neglect, 12,* 529-541.

LaFave, W. R., & Israel, J. H. (1991). *Criminal procedure* (2nd ed). St. Paul, MN: West.

Landeros v. Flood, 551 P.2d 389 (Cal. 1976).

Lanktree, C., Briere, J., & Zaidi, L. (1991). Incidence and impact of sexual abuse in a child outpatient sample: The role of direct inquiry. *Child Abuse & Neglect, 15,* 447-453.

Lehman v. Stephens, 499 N.E.2d 103 (Ill. Ct. App. 1986).

Libow, J. A., & Schreier, H. A. (1986). Three forms of factitious illness in children: When is it Munchausen syndrome by proxy? *American Journal of Orthopsychiatry, 56,* 602-611.

Lilly, G. C. (1987). *An introduction to the law of evidence.* St. Paul, MN: West.

Lindsay, D. S., & Johnson, M. K. (1987). Reality monitoring and suggestibility: Children's ability to discriminate among memories from different sources. In S. J. Ceci, M. P. Toglia, & D. F. Ross (Eds.), *Children's eyewitness memory* (pp. 92-121). New York: Springer-Verlag.

Lipovsky, J. A., Saunders, B. E., & Murphy, S. M. (1989). Depression, anxiety, and behavior problems among victims of father-child sexual assault and nonabused siblings. *Journal of Interpersonal Violence, 4,* 452-468.

Louisell, D. W., & Mueller, C. B. (1979). *Federal evidence* (Vol. 3). San Francisco: Bancroft-Whitney.

Lovett v. Superior Court, 250 Cal. Rptr. 25 (Ct. App. 1988).

MacFarlane, K., & Waterman, J. (1986). *Sexual abuse of young children.* New York: Guilford.

Mannarino, A. P., & Cohen, J. A. (1986). A clinical-demographic study of sexually abused children. *Child Abuse & Neglect, 10,* 17-23.

Maples v. Siddiqui, 450 N.W.2d 529 (Iowa 1990).

Markman, E. M. (1977). Realizing that you don't understand: A preliminary investigation. *Child Development, 48,* 986-992.

Markman, E. M. (1979). Realizing that you don't understand: Elementary school children's awareness of inconsistencies. *Child Development, 50,* 643-655.

Martin v. Weld County, 598 P.2d 532 (Colo. Ct. App. 1979).

Maryland v. Craig, 110 S.Ct. 3157 (1990).

Matter of Appeal in Cochise County Juvenile Action, 650 P.2d 459 (Ariz. 1982).

Matter of Appeal in Pima County Juvenile Dependency Action No. 96290, 785 P.2d 121 (Ariz. Ct. App. 1990).

Matter of Dull, 521 N.E.2d 972 (Ind. Ct. App. 1988).

Matter of Schmeltzer, 438 N.W.2d 866 (Mich. Ct. App. 1989).

Matter of T.C., 784 P.2d 392 (Mont. 1989).

Matthews, E., & Saywitz, K. J. (1992). Child victim witness manual. *California Center for Judicial Education and Research Journal, 12,* 5-81.

McCormick on Evidence (3rd ed.). (1984). E. W. Cleary (Ed.). St. Paul, MN: West.

Mehl, A. L., Coble, L., & Johnson, S. (1990). Munchausen syndrome by proxy: A family affair. *Child Abuse & Neglect, 14,* 577-585.

Meinig, M. B. (1991). Profile of Roland Summit [Interview]. *Violence Update, 1*(9), 6-7.

Melton, G. B. (1981). Children's competence to testify. *Law & Human Behavior, 5,* 73-85.

Melton, G. B., & Limber, S. (1989). Psychologists' involvement in cases of child maltreatment. *American Psychologist, 44,* 1225-1233.

Melton, G. B., Petrila, J., Poythress, N., & Slobogin, C. (1987). *Psychological evaluations for the courts.* New York: Guilford.

Miranda v. Arizona, 384 U.S. 436 (1966).

Morgan v. Foretich, 846 F.2d 941 (4th Cir. 1988).

Moss, D. C. (1988). Abuse scale: Point system for abuse claims. *American Bar Association Journal, 74*(12), 26.

Mosteller, R. P. (1989). Child sexual abuse and statements for the purpose of medical diagnosis or treatment. *North Carolina Law Review, 67,* 257-294.

Murphy, J. M., Jellinek, M., Quinn, D., Smith, G., Poitrast, F. G., & Goshko, M. (1991). Substance abuse and serious child mistreatment: Prevalence, risk, and outcome in a court sample. *Child Abuse & Neglect, 15,* 197-211.

Myers, J. E. B. (1990). The child sexual abuse literature: A call for greater objectivity. *Michigan Law Review, 88,* 1709-1733.

Myers, J. E. B. (1992). *Evidence in child abuse and neglect cases.* New York: Wiley Law Publications.

Myers, J. E. B. (in press). Expert testimony regarding child sexual abuse. *Child Abuse & Neglect.*

Myers, J. E. B., Bays, J., Becker, J., Berliner, L., Corwin, D., & Saywitz, K. (1989). Expert testimony in child sexual abuse litigation. *Nebraska Law Review, 68*, 1-34.

Myers, J. E. B., & Peters, W. D. (1987). *Child abuse reporting legislation in the 1980s.* Denver, CO: American Humane Association.

National Association of Social Workers. (1980). *Code of ethics.* Washington, DC: Author.

Nelson, K. (1986). *Event knowledge: Structure and function in development.* Hillsdale, NJ: Lawrence Erlbaum.

New York v. Ferber, 458 U.S. 747 (1982).

Nye, S. G. (1980). Legal issues in the practice of child psychiatry. In D. H. Schetky & E. P. Benedek (Eds.), *Child psychiatry and the law* (pp. 266-286). New York: Brunner/Mazel.

Ochs, E., & Schieflin, B. (1979). *Developmental pragmatics.* New York: Academic Press.

Orenstein, D. M., & Wasserman, A. L. (1986). Munchausen syndrome by proxy simulating cystic fibrosis. *Pediatrics, 78*, 621-624.

Patterson, C. J., Massad, C. M., & Cosgrove, J. M. (1978). Children's referential communication: Components of plans for effective listening. *Developmental Psychology, 14*, 401-406.

Payne v. State, 731 S.W.2d 235 (Ark. 1987).

Pennsylvania v. Ritchie, 480 U.S. 39 (1987).

People v. Bledsoe, 681 P.2d 291 (Cal. 1984).

People v. Bowker, 249 Cal. Rptr. 886 (1988).

People v. Coleman, 768 P.2d 32 (Cal. 1989).

People v. D.A.K., 596 P.2d 747 (Colo. 1979).

People v. Hampton, 746 P.2d 947 (Colo. 1987).

People v. Harp, 550 N.E.2d 1163 (Ill. Ct. App. 1990).

People v. McAlpin, 812 P.2d 563 (Cal. 1991).

People v. Mendibles, 245 Cal. Rptr. 553 (1988).

People v. Phillips, 175 Cal. Rptr. 703 (1981).

People v. Stoll, 783 P.2d 698 (Cal. 1989).

People v. Taylor, 552 N.E.2d 131, 552 N.Y.S.2d 883 (1990).

Perry, N. W. (1987). Child and adolescent development: A psycholegal perspective. In J. E. B. Myers, *Child witness law and practice* (pp. 459-525). New York: Wiley Law Publications.

Perry, N. W., & Wrightsman, L. S. (1991). *The child witness: Legal issues and dilemmas.* Newbury Park, CA: Sage.

Peters, D. P. (1987). The impact of naturally occurring stress on children's memory. In S. J. Ceci, M. P. Toglia & D. F. Ross (Eds.), *Children's eyewitness memory* (pp. 122-141). New York: Springer-Verlag.

Peters, D. P. (1991). The influence of stress and arousal on the child witness. In J. Doris (Ed.), *The suggestibility of children's recollections* (pp. 60-76). Washington, DC: American Psychological Association.

Petition of Catholic Charitable Bureau of Archdiocese of Boston, 479 N.E.2d 148 (Mass. 1985).

President's Commission on Law Enforcement and Administration of Justice. (1968). *The challenge of crime in a free society.* New York: Avon.

Prince v. Massachusetts, 321 U.S. 158 (1944).

Pynoos, R. S., & Eth, S. (1984). The child as witness to homicide. *Journal of Social Issues, 40*, 87-108.

Quinn, K. M. (1988). The credibility of children's allegations of sexual abuse. *Behavioral Science & Law, 6*, 181-199.

Rabinowitz, D. (1990, May). From the mouths of babes to a jail cell. Child abuse and the abuse of justice: A case study. *Harper's Magazine*, pp. 52-63.

Raskin, D. C., & Esplin, P. W. (1991). Assessment of children's statements of sexual abuse. In J. Doris (Ed.), *The suggestibility of children's recollections* (pp. 153-164). Washington, DC: American Psychological Association.

Raskin, D. C., & Yuille, J. C. (1989). Problems in evaluating interviews of children in sexual abuse cases. In S. J. Ceci, D. F. Ross, & M. P. Toglia (Eds.), *Perspectives on children's testimony* (pp. 184-207). New York: Springer-Verlag.

Reuben and Elizabeth O. v. Department of Human Services, 725 P.2d 844 (N.M. Ct. App. 1986).

Reynolds v. United States, 98 U.S. 145 (1878).

Rheingold, P. D. (1962). The basis of medical testimony. *Vanderbilt Law Review, 15*, 473-534.

Russell, D. E. H. (1983). The incidence and prevalence of intrafamilial and extrafamilial sexual abuse of female children. *Child Abuse & Neglect, 7*, 133-146.

Russell, D. E. H. (1986a). *Intrafamily child sexual abuse: A San Francisco survey* (Final Report to the National Center on Child Abuse and Neglect).

Russell, D. E. H. (1986b). *The secret trauma: Incest in the lives of girls and women*. New York: Basic Books.

Russell v. Texas Department of Human Resources, 746 S.W.2d 510 (Tex. App. 1988).

Salter, A. C. (1991). *Accuracy of expert testimony in child sexual abuse cases: A case study of Ralph Underwager and Holida Wakefield*. Alexandria, VA: National Center for the Prosecution of Child Abuse.

Salter v. Larsen, 520 N.Y.S.2d 378 (A.D. 1987).

Santosky v. Kramer, 455 U.S. 745 (1982).

Saywitz, K. J. (1989). Children's conceptions of the legal system: "Court is a place to play basketball." In S. J. Ceci, D. F. Ross, & M. P. Toglia (Eds.), *Perspectives on children's testimony* (pp. 131-157). New York: Springer-Verlag.

Saywitz, K. J., Geiselman, R. E., & Bornstein, G. K. (in press). Effects of cognitive interviewing and practice on children's recall performance. *Journal of Applied Psychology*.

Saywitz, K. J., Goodman, G. S., & Myers, J. E. B. (1990). Can children provide accurate eyewitness reports? *Violence Update, 1*(1) 3,9.

Saywitz, K. J., Goodman, G. S., Nicholas, E., & Moan, S. F. (1991). Children's memories of physical examinations involving genital touch: Implications for reports of child sexual abuse. *Journal of Consulting & Clinical Psychology, 59*, 682-691.

Saywitz, K. J., Jaenicke, C., & Camparo, L. (1990). Children's knowledge of legal terminology. *Law & Human Behavior, 14*, 523-535.

Saywitz, K. J., Moan, S., & Lamphear, V. (1991, August). *The effects of preparation on children's resistance to misleading questions*. Paper presented at annual meeting of the American Psychological Association, San Francisco.

Saywitz, K. J., & Nathanson, R. (in press). Children's testimony and perceived stress in and out of the courtroom. *Child Abuse & Neglect*.

Saywitz, K. J., & Snyder, L. (in press). Improving children's testimony with preparation. In G. S. Goodman & B. L. Bottoms (Eds.), *Understanding and improving children's testimony*. New York: Guilford.

Schmitt, B. D. (1987). The child with nonaccidental trauma. In R. E. Helfer & R. S. Kempe (Eds.), *The battered child* (pp. 178-196). Chicago: University of Chicago Press.

Schmitt, B. D., & Mauro, R. D. (1989). Nonorganic failure to thrive: An outpatient approach. *Child Abuse & Neglect, 13,* 235-248.

Seering v. Department of Social Services, 239 Cal. Rptr. 422 (Ct. App. 1987).

Selman, R. L., & Byrne, D. (1974). A structural developmental analysis of levels of role taking in middle childhood. *Child Development, 45,* 803-806.

Sgroi, S. M., Porter, F. S., & Blick, L. C. (1982). Validation of child sexual abuse. In S. M. Sgroi (Ed.), *Handbook of clinical intervention in child sexual abuse* (pp. 39-79). Lexington, MA: Lexington.

Shannon v. State, 783 P.2d 942 (Nev. 1989).

Sharon H. v. Foster, 544 N.Y.S.2d 659 (A.D. 1989).

Singer, D., & Revenson, T. (1978). *How a child thinks.* New York: Plume.

Singer, J. B., & Flavell, J. H. (1981). Children's evaluations of explicitly ambiguous messages. *Child Development, 52,* 1211-1215.

Sivan, A. B. (1991). Preschool child development: Implications for investigation of child abuse allegations. *Child Abuse & Neglect, 15,* 485-493.

Sorensen, T., & Snow, B. (1991). How children tell: The process of disclosure in child sexual abuse. *Child Welfare, 70,* 3-15.

Spencer, J. R., & Flin, R. (1990). *The evidence of children: The law and the psychology.* London: Blackstone.

State v. Allewalt, 517 A.2d 741 (Md. 1986).

State v. Black, 745 P.2d 12 (Wash. 1987).

State v. Brodniak, 718 P.2d 322 (Mont. 1986).

State v. Charles, 398 S.E.2d 123 (W. Va. 1990).

State v. Gettier, 438 N.W.2d 1 (Iowa 1989).

State v. Graham, 798 P.2d 314 (Wash. Ct. App. 1990).

State v. Hester, 760 P.2d 27 (Idaho 1988).

State v. Huey, 699 P.2d 1290 (Ariz. 1985).

State v. Jensen, 432 N.W.2d (Wis. 1988).

State v. Lamb, 427 N.W.2d 142 (Wis. 1988).

State v. Lindsey, 720 P.2d 73 (Ariz. 1986).

State v. Logan, 806 P.2d 137 (Or. 1991).

State v. Marks, 647 P.2d 1292 (Kan. 1982).

State v. McCoy, 366 S.E.2d 731 (W. Va. 1988).

State v. Milbradt, 756 P.2d 620 (Or. 1988).

State v. Moran, 728 P.2d 248 (Ariz. 1986).

State v. Person, 564 A.2d 626 (Conn. Ct. App. 1989).

State v. Phelps, 696 P.2d 447 (Mont. 1985).

State v. Rimmasch, 775 P.2d 388 (Utah 1989).

State v. Schimpf, 782 S.W.2d 186 (Tenn. Crim. App. 1989).

Strichartz, A. F., & Burton, R. V. (1990). Lies and truth: A study of the development of the concept. *Child Development, 61,* 211-220.

Summit, R. C. (1983). The child sexual abuse accommodation syndrome. *Child Abuse & Neglect, 7,* 177-193.

Summit, R. C. (1988). Hidden victims, hidden pain: Societal avoidance of child sexual abuse. In G. E. Wyatt & G. J. Powell (Eds.), *Lasting effects of child sexual abuse* (pp. 39-60). Newbury Park, CA: Sage.

Tarasoff v. Regents of the University of California, 529 P.2d 553 (Cal. 1974).

Taylor v. Ledbetter, 818 F.2d 791 (11th Cir. 1987).

Thomas v. Chadwick, 274 Cal. Rptr. 128 (Ct. App. 1990).

Terr, L. C. (1988). What happens to early memories of trauma? A study of twenty children under age five at the time of documented traumatic events. *Journal of the American Academy of Child and Adolescent Psychiatry, 27,* 96-104.

Tobey, A. E., & Goodman, G. S. (in press). Children's eyewitness memory: Effects of participation and forensic context. *Child Abuse & Neglect.*

Turner v. District of Columbia, 532 A.2d 662 (D.C. 1987).

Tymchuk, A. J., & Andron, L. (1990). Mothers with mental retardation who do or do not abuse or neglect their children. *Child Abuse & Neglect, 14,* 313-323.

United States v. Azure, 801 F.2d 336 (8th Cir. 1986).

United States v. Barnard, 490 F.2d 907 (9th Cir. 1973).

United States v. Carter, 26 M.J. 428 (C.M.A. 1988).

United States v. Gillespie, 852 F.2d 475 (9th Cir. 1988).

United States v. Gordon-Nikkar, 518 F.2d 972 (5th Cir. 1975).

United States v. Iron Shell, 633 F.2d 77 (8th Cir. 1980).

Vissing, Y. M., Straus, M. A., Gelles, R. J., & Harrop, J. W. (1991). Verbal aggression by parents and psychological problems of children. *Child Abuse & Neglect, 15,* 223-238.

Vosburg v. Department of Social Services, 884 F.2d 133 (4th Cir. 1989).

Wakefield, H., & Underwager, R. (1988). *Accusations of child sexual abuse.* Springfield, IL: Charles C Thomas.

Warren, A., Hulse-Trotter, K., & Tubbs, E. C. (1991). Inducing resistance to suggestibility in children. *Law & Human Behavior, 15,* 273-285.

Wells, G. L., & Loftus, E. F. (1991). Commentary: Is this child fabricating? Reactions to a new assessment technique. In J. Doris (Ed.), *The suggestibility of children's recollections* (pp. 168-171). Washington, DC: American Psychological Association.

Whitcomb, D., Runyan, D. K., De Vos, E., Hunter, W. M., Cross, T. P., Everson, M. D., Peeler, N. A., Porter, C. Q., Toth, P. A., & Cropper, C. (1991). *Final report* (Child Victim as Witness Research and Development Program, Grant No. 87-MC-CX-0026, U.S. Department of Justice, Office of Justice Programs, Office of Juvenile Justice and Delinquency Prevention).

White, S., & Quinn, K. M. (1988). Investigatory independence in child sexual abuse evaluations: Conceptual considerations. *Bulletin of the American Academy of Psychiatry and Law, 16,* 269-278.

Wigmore, J. (1974). *Evidence in trials at common law.* Boston: Little, Brown.

Williams, R. A. (1991). Injuries in infants and small children resulting from witnessed and corroborated free falls. *Journal of Trauma, 31,* 1350-1352.

Wisconsin v. Yoder, 406 U.S. 205 (1972).

Wozencraft, T., Wagner, W., & Pellegrin, A. (1991). Depression and suicidal ideation in sexually abused children. *Child Abuse & Neglect, 15,* 505-511.

Wyatt, G. E., & Powell, G. J. (Eds.). (1988). *Lasting effects of child sexual abuse.* Newbury Park, CA: Sage.

Yates, A., & Musty, T. (1988). Preschool children's erroneous allegations of sexual molestation. *American Journal of Psychiatry, 145,* 989-992.

Zaragoza, M. S. (1987). Memory, suggestibility, and eyewitness testimony in children and adults. In S. J. Ceci, M. P. Toglia, & D. F. Ross (Eds.), *Children's eyewitness memory* (pp. 53-78). New York: Springer-Verlag.

Zellman, G. L. (1990). Report decision-making patterns among mandated child abuse reporters. *Child Abuse & Neglect, 14,* 325-336.

Zumwalt, R. E., & Hirsch, C. S. (1987). Pathology of fatal child abuse and neglect. In R. E. Helfer & R. S. Kempe (Eds.), *The battered child* (pp. 247-285). Chicago: University of Chicago Press.

Index

About the Author

John E. B. Myers, J.D., is Professor of Law at the University of the Pacific, McGeorge School of Law, in Sacramento, California. He is nationally recognized as an expert on investigation and litigation of child abuse and neglect. He is the author of numerous books and articles discussing legal issues in child abuse and neglect, and his writings have been cited by more than 70 courts, including the U.S. Supreme Court and numerous state supreme courts. In addition to his writing and teaching, he is a frequent speaker at conferences on child abuse.